RITA'S TRANSFORMATION

Rita Murray

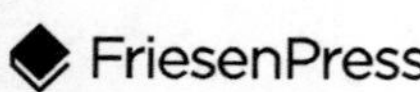

One Printers Way
Altona, MB R0G 0B0
Canada

www.friesenpress.com

First Edition — 2022

Illustrator: Jeanette Bégin

ISBN
978-1-03-913822-3 (Hardcover)
978-1-03-913821-6 (Paperback)
978-1-03-913823-0 (eBook)

1. RELIGION, CHRISTIAN LIFE, INSPIRATIONAL

Distributed to the trade by The Ingram Book Company

Romans 12:2 *"Be transformed by the renewal of your mind, so that you may prove what is the good and acceptable and perfect will of God, even the thing which is good and acceptable and perfect."*

This book is dedicated to
My Lord Jesus Christ
who has inspired me
and has brought to mind a lot of the incidents in my life,
and has been with me throughout the writing of it.

Thanks go to the friends who had encouraged me,
helped me along the way.

Note: Part of proceeds from the sale of this book will
go to
Harvest House Drug and Alcohol Rehabilitation.

Table of Contents

Introduction

Besides events in my life, as I see it, my story will tell you a little about what I *was* like, what happened and what I am like now. Some of those key events explore memories of: how I was delivered from the fear of thunder and lightning; going over bridges; shyness; jealousy, stemmed from my own insecurities; being a smoker of cigarettes, and a hoarder of 'things'. I will tell you about dealing and changing from being an angry person; being a master controller; of negativity thinking; trust; taking revenge; hate; and being self-absorbed, to name a few.

Also explored in these pages is my learning on changing my way of talking differently by changing some of the words I say like, "I can't" to "I can"; "Yes," only if I mean Yes, and, "No," if I mean No; to compliment people when I get the opportunity…just to name a few.

In the chapters that follow, I will reveal what I did to change from old patterns of behaviour to what I do now instead. There is still lots of changing for me to do. I am never going to be perfect but that is what I have been striving for. I know I will never get 'there' but trying my best to do so. I am not where I want to be yet but I have come a long way from where I used to be.

You will read a lot about God in my story. This book is being written because I believe it was God who told me to write it and I am depending on Him to be able to do so.

All events are true as I saw them and still remember them, but most of the names have been changed to protect those individuals.

Chapter 1
DEATH BY FIRE

It all started during WWII in 1944 when Dad was home on leave from the army and was at his second cousin's home. My dad and maternal grandmother were second cousins. The following year in 1945 just about a month before the end of the war, I was born in my grandparents' home. Mom and Dad were not married and, in those days, unwed, pregnant women were disapproved of and frowned upon. Mom was only eighteen years old and my dad was thirty-six years old. I was born in July and they got married in August.

Still living at her parents' home, Mom was expected to continue doing all the housework as she had been doing before I was born. She wasn't well, and by the time she had the housework done, there was no time left nor was she able to take care of me properly. My dad thought it was best to get us out of there and rented a one-room shack to have a place of our own. They put up a sheet to separate the bedroom and the rest of the living space. I remember a wood stove, a stack of wood beside it, a table in the living space, and three beds in the bedroom—one for Mom and Dad, one for my brothers and I, and a baby crib.

The well where water was drawn from was way down in the field behind the barn. It didn't have a pump to pump up the water. Mom had to let a pail tied to a long rope down into the well to bring up the water and then carry it to the house. Can you imagine the water she needed to wash all our clothes, for cooking and drinking? Today we just turn a tap on and out comes the water.

Dad's job was working in the bush cutting wood with an axe. I remember him sharpening it before he went to work in the morning and whittling an axe handle so he can cut down the trees.

When I was in high school and taking the bus, we drove pass that one-room shack and picked up a boy who lived on that property. I told him that I lived in the small house beside the large one. He told me that the small 'house' was the wood shed, not a house. I couldn't believe that someone would be using my first home as a wood shed. I told my mom after school that night that the people living there had built a large house beside ours and used ours for a wood shed. She already knew all about it.

We had a small border collie named Rex. I would climb up holding onto Rex and he would walk slowly as I walked along beside him. That was how I learned to walk. He was my constant companion until he crossed the road one day and went into the field on the other side. There, a neighbour from down the road, was hunting on that property and shot and killed my pet.

My grandpa died when I was only four years old. The only times I remember of him was me sitting on his knees and the next time he was laying on the bed in the living room. I was allowed to sit on the bed beside him with Dad beside me. The next time was my grandpa 'sleeping' in a different but very high bed in the middle of the living room. I climbed up to the bed and laid down beside him. I was the only one in the room at the time. My granny came in and yelled at me because I was laying down beside grandpa. My dad must have heard her and came in and took me down from the high bed. When I was older, I was told that the high bed was a coffin. Everyone had been saying that grandpa was 'sleeping' instead of saying that he was dead. I didn't know what they meant. I probably wouldn't have understood what dead was anyway. He was being waked in the living room of their home, which I understand now; many times, that was what they did in those days. Mom never really could enjoy Christmas after that because he was buried on Christmas day. I don't know how they did that because of the frozen ground but I was told that was the day that he was buried.

Two Brothers, Arthur and Oscar and a sister, Anna, were born in this shack. I don't remember my sister in that shack but I know she was born there. I remember pouring baby powder on my brother Oscar's hair and when I was a little bit older, I noticed that his hair was blond, almost white, and the rest of us all had dark hair. For a long time, I thought it was white because I had poured the baby powder on him, until Mom explained that it wasn't.

I was about three or four years old when we moved from there to one side of a double house on a farm. Here, I remember not being very happy because the landlady didn't want us to play outside for some reason. Her children played outside but we weren't allowed to. I do remember we sneaked into the barn on the property and played in it one afternoon without her catching us outside. That was the best afternoon I had outside at that place except when the landlord was home. I didn't like that woman at all. The landlord—when he was home which wasn't often—we all liked. He was kind and would take us out to play when he took his own kids out.

Another brother, William, was born while living in this house. My mother was taken to the hospital by horse-drawn sleigh through snow-bound roads that nothing else could go down. When they got home from the hospital, I remember wanting my mother to bring the baby back to where she got him from. I thought he was so ugly—he did grow up to be quite good looking though. I didn't know, because I was too young to understand, that it wasn't the hospital that gave him to her. Of course, she didn't give him back.

The day we moved from there, sitting down to have our last meal in the kitchen with the table in front of the window, the landlady's children were making fun of us through that window. I didn't know why they were making fun of us or why I felt so ashamed. I have not liked anyone looking at me while I eat since. I don't mind if they are eating but if they just sit there and watch me, I feel uncomfortable.

I also had an aunt, who was burned and died in a barn fire. Every time granny would give me a ribbon for my hair or something that used to belong to her, she would say, "This used to belong to your Aunt Rita; she died in a barn fire, you know." How could I not know, I heard it so often. It got to be that I didn't want anything from granny if it had belonged to my Aunt Rita. I had never known her and definitely didn't want to hear about her being burned in a fire. I think that is why I became afraid of fire and would burn myself every time I got near the wood stove to do something. Mom also thought so. She mentioned it to me one day when we were talking about it. My aunt had been only four years old and she and my Uncle Bob had been playing in the hayloft. He was too young to know to get her out but he did run to the house to let someone know that the barn was on fire. Everyone suspected that he had been playing with matches in the hayloft.

Chapter 2
Spiced Cake

The next place we moved to was to a large farm house with a very kind landlord. He would come visit often to check up on us to see if everything was OK. He knew Mom was not in good health and raising all us kids would need extra help when Dad was away at work. It was a good thing that he did because one day he showed up just in time to put out a fire in the old sleigh that was in the carriage house at the back of the property. Arthur and I were at school and Mom wasn't able to look after the others at home because she was sick in bed. I shudder to think what could have happened if he hadn't come to check on her and the kids.

Another day we came home to find that Oscar had gotten a pair of moms' sewing scissors and had cut up Anna's hair. What a mess.

My sister Pauline was born here and was named after our doctor except made into a girl's name. Doctors in those days made house calls and she, like most of us, was born at home. Mom was sick in bed for a long time when she was born.

Dad got a relative to come and stay with us and look after Mom and us kids and to do the housework. Being young, she took advantage and made some of us older ones empty the potty pail that she used. I don't remember if she stayed long. I have never seen her since.

I was a bleeder. I remember being on my back on the couch and Dad putting a cold cloth on my forehead and a large set of keys on my chest. This was to stop the nose bleeding. I was told it was an old Indian remedy. This would happen often. As I got older the bleeding wasn't as often but I still had to be careful. I got nose bleeds easily.

I remember two rooms off the living room that were the bedrooms in the winter time. One was Mom and Dad's room and the other had one large bed for us kids. We all slept in that one bed. While here I had the chicken pox and the measles at the same time. I got it first and the others after me. I wasn't allowed to walk on the floor so I would get up on a chair, walk the chair to another and place the chairs so that I could go all around the living room without touching the floor. Mom didn't want me to get sick again by touching the cold floor.

In the summer we slept upstairs. We had a bed for the girls and one for the boys in a larger room. Mom and Dad had their bedroom at the other end of the hallway. The stairs had a door at the bottom with a keyhole. When Dad would get up to go to work, I would sneak down the stairs and peak through that keyhole to watch him eat his breakfast. He was gone so early and home so late that we hardly saw him during the week at all. We were lucky if we saw him on weekends. He left early because he had to walk into the city to go to work and walk back at night. It was a long walk.

Our favourite places to play were in the old barn and in the hay. My lone spot was in the old granary above the shed. I would take a catalogue and cut out pictures of people and clothing and dress them up with the paper clothing. I spent hours in that granary. In the summertime, there was a honey bee's nest in the logs of the granary wall and my brothers and sister wouldn't come near it so I knew they wouldn't disturb me.

The first time I saw a wolf was in the adjacent field to the barn. Being in the evening, Dad was home from work and he told us that the wolf was trying to get to our chickens. If he wasn't home, we were to go inside until he came home. I knew then that a wolf was not a friendly animal. The next time I saw a wolf was when my friend's girlfriend came to visit with her pet wolf. That wolf seemed to be tame and friendly. The girl kept it on a leash. She had raised it from a small pup.

Also, we saw our sow with sun stroke. At least that is what Dad told us. I have looked up what sun stroke is like on pigs but can't find any pig's behaviour like we saw ours doing. She had broken out of her pen and was attacking everything and hitting her head on things. She was in such pain. We were told to stay inside for our safety. We were also told that the only way to get her out of her pain was to put her down.

I hated bandy roosters since I was about five years old. We had a nasty one that liked to attack people and one day as I was walking to the barn, he attacked me. Being so small he got the best of me and I fell down on the ground giving him the advantage to peck and scratch my face and everywhere he could. I yelled and yelled for Mom but she was across the road at the neighbour's and didn't hear me. I yelled until I couldn't get any sound out. Eventually the rooster quit and I was able to go see Mom.

One night that rooster got its due reward. I was so glad. A friend of Mom and Dad's came calling and the rooster attacked him. He reached down, grabbed it by the neck and yanked it hard enough to break its neck. The friend came to the door with the rooster hanging in his hands and said, "He won't attack anyone ever again." We did have more bandy hens on the farm but never had problems with them.

Dad didn't go to work one Saturday. Mom and Dad were still in bed so my brother Arthur and I decided to go to the creek to catch fish for our breakfast. We had been told not to go to the creek, that it was dangerous. Dad came over the hill and saw us at the creek. He didn't ask any questions. We had disobeyed. Thinking we could outrun 'the old man' figuring that he was too old to run we started running home across the field. Never tried that one again! He caught up with us before we got half way across that field and booted us all the way home yelling at us as he did it. It was explained later that they were worried when we weren't at the house and no one answered when they called.

One day Mom was doing her washing outside. It was a ringer washer that she had to fill with water, scrub the clothing on the washboard to wash, and then put the washed clothing through the wringer by turning the handle. The clothes would then go into a laundry tub on the other side of the wringer to be rinsed. She drew water from the outside pump and brought it into the house, put it in a tub on the wood stove to heat up.

When it was hot, she would have to bring it out to put in the laundry tub of the washing machine. Put in the soap and scrub the clothes by hand to wash them. She would also have to pump the water to put in the tub to rinse the clothes. She would rinse the clothes and put them through the ringer again into a basket so she can go hang them on the line. When she had done that load, she went into the house to get another load of clothes to wash. I was playing nearby watching her.

While she was in the house, I decided to wash my dirty bull frog I was playing with. Being too young to understand I put him in the tub to wash. It went well, then I put him in the ringer and turned the handle like my mom had done. It didn't go so well! My poor pet frog was crushed. Mom came out and saw the mess I had done. Instead of yelling at me she seemed to understand what I was trying to do. She soothed me and told me that it doesn't work on frogs as it does with clothing. She had to clean up the mess I had done, then pump more water, warm it up, refill the tubs, before finishing her washing. A long and hard job the first time without having to clean up and start again.

In the wintertime, she would do the washing in the house. The washing machine would be brought into the kitchen and water was drawn from the well to heat up on the wood stove and then was put into the washing machine and the laundry tub. The laundry tub would be put on a chair to prevent the splashing of water onto the floor. She would hang the clothing on the outside line. A lot of times when she would bring in the clothing it would be frozen and have to be hung up until the freezing thawed and the clothes were dried before being ironed and put away.

I remember that Christmas and New Year's were happy ones there. Christmas was at granny's house but New Year's was at our house. All the relatives would come for a meal and stay late into the night, playing cards, dancing and just enjoying each other.

When it was near Christmas time, we would all gather around the radio and listen to Santa Claus, Mary, and Grackle. It was the highlight of our days. Also, during the year, we would listen to plays like "Boston Blackie", "The Third Man", "The Shadow" and others, on that old battery radio. It was just a small battery radio but we were fortunate to have one. There was no electricity in most of the homes - at least the ones we knew – back then.

Another day my brother Arthur and I decided to make a cake. We had watched Mom baking cakes many times. I remember we both knew what the first two or three ingredients were but when it came to spices, we were not so sure. Arthur would point to one—we had all the spices on the table—and said, "I think she put this one in," and we would pour some in the batter. I picked the next one and put some of that one in. We finished putting in all the spices we thought Mom had put in her cakes. Mixed it all and put it in the pan and then the oven. Relatives were coming for supper that night and the cake was served as desert. Everyone raved about how good it was. Then Mom told them that she hadn't baked it, that Arthur and I had done it without her supervision. God was with us that day, that we hadn't put in the wrong spices. For instance, poultry seasoning and other spices that didn't go in baked goods, on the table. We were too young to know the difference. Also, some of the spices that we did put in the cake, Mom would put in *different* cakes, not all in the same cake. I tried to bake another cake many times after that but we hadn't written anything down so I never was able to duplicate it.

Aunt May, Mom's sister, was dating a man named Tom. Uncle Louis, Mom's brother, was dating a woman named Alice. We used to call them Uncle and Aunt because we figured they would become our aunt and uncle. When my aunt May started going out with someone else and my uncle Louis did the same, we never stopped saying Uncle Tom and Aunt Alice. As it turned out they were married together and stayed around. It was not until I was an older teenager that I realized that they were not related and not my aunt and uncle.

These were the two that I used to babysit for when I was a teenager. He taught me how to dance the "two step" as Mom had taught him. I only found that out when one day when I was teaching his oldest son how to do it. They came home from shopping for groceries and found us all dancing and that is when he told me that Mom had taught him. Today, that would probably be called 'what goes around comes around.'

The first wedding I remember going to was my Uncle Louis and Aunt Mary's wedding. I really liked his girlfriend and she became one of my favourite aunts. She had been raised in an orphan home and had no one else for family. The day that they came back from their honeymoon, they came to visit. Uncle Louis came in with his arms around both his new wife and another woman. He came in and introduced them, "This is my girlfriend—this is my wife." I took immediate offence to it. As young as I was, I knew he should not have a girlfriend nor have his arm around her. What made it worse for me was that he introduced his girlfriend first before my Aunt Mary and the girlfriend being a redhead didn't help. I didn't like redheads at the time. The girlfriend then proceeded to place her attention on me and tried to make me her friend, but I was having none of it. This did not change with my uncle. Up to his second-last wife, he always had a girlfriend, on the side, and took them into his home with his wives. I had no respect for him.

When they had children, I used to babysit for her. I would visit often but it usually was when he wasn't home. One night when he was out, Aunt Mary and I were fooling around and I said, "He's probably out with another woman." I didn't believe it but when he got home, we could see lipstick on his shirt collar. I told my aunt that I didn't mean it and told her I was sorry. I could see that she was hurting.

They lived about five miles from our place and I would usually walk home even though it was dark out. After a night of babysitting, if Uncle Louis came home first and wanted to drive me home, I didn't trust him enough to get into his car with him alone to drive me home. I had to fight him off a few times before when my aunt wasn't home after a babysitting evening. I remember one night in the winter time, it was really cold out. I went next door from their place to ask if someone could drive me home. I didn't have to explain why. They knew what he was like. Some of my babysitting money was used to buy a padlock for the inside of my cousin's bedroom door to keep him out of it. He wasn't too happy about that but she did lock it when she went to sleep. Today I realize that he is a very sick man and he was back then; but I didn't know that it is a sickness.

Chapter 3
PICTURE RADIO

My father used to buy us a pail of hard candies every Christmas time. One year he bought two. The second one was for a family who couldn't afford any candy for Christmas. He also told us that the angels would know who to bring it to and they would bring the second one to a household that couldn't afford any. I felt rich. From that, I learned that there were people less fortunate than we were. On the next morning, after my father was gone to work, and everyone else including my mom was still in bed, I went downstairs to check. The pail of candies was still in the cupboard! I was so disappointed. I ran back up to my mom's room and told her that the angels had not picked it up. She said it was gone, go check again. Arthur (up by this time) and I went down to check like she said. It was gone! To this day I still don't know how. I've asked my mother years later and all she said was the angel picked it up. I have tried through the years to figure it out but couldn't.

Just before another Christmas a salesman came to the door and showed Mom what he was selling. Mom bought four different plaster plaques in the shape of horses in horseshoe wall hangings. Three were for us, and one for granny. The one for granny was to be delivered by an angel so granny wouldn't know where it came from. At least that is what we were told. On Christmas morning, it was still at our place but when I walked in the door at granny's place, I saw it hanging on her wall. I asked how it got there and granny said that she didn't know. Again, how did it get to granny's place before we did? Just another mystery from my childhood.

Dad used to tell us a story from his youth, that one Sunday afternoon he was with his friends and a knock came at the door. The owner went outside to talk to a well-dressed and handsome man. They heard their friend yelling but when they went out to check, he wasn't there. A few weeks went by. He finally showed up again on a Sunday afternoon when they were all together again. His clothes were all torn up, his arms, hands and face were scratched but when asked where he had been and what happened, all he told them was, he had been to hell and back. He never said anymore about it. My dad explained that this man had done a lot of bad things besides a lot of drinking before and stopped all of it afterwards and never drank again. He believed that it was the devil who had come to the door that day.

My dad would tell us this especially when one of us did wrong. He didn't want the devil to come get us.

I learned at an early age that the devil can appear to be nice but wasn't and we were to be good if we wanted to go to heaven and be with Jesus. At times it did stop me from doing bad but at other times not so much. Later on in years, I completely forgot that story. Was it true? Or was it just Dad's way to help us to be good instead of doing bad things that would not have been good for us. It doesn't matter, it did the job, mostly.

That is when Dad quit drinking too. He used to swear an oath on the Bible once a year not to get drunk for the following year. When I was about seventeen or eighteen years old, he went to a stag and had to be driven home. The neighbour who drove him home brought him to pick up his car the next day. He drank every day—as far as I know—after that.

When I met my husband-to-be, my dad and he became the best of buddies and drank together. I learned early in their relationship that I better not say anything against him because Dad would take his side every time. When Dad drank, he was a much nicer person than when he didn't drink. When he wasn't drinking, I never knew when he might get angry and hit us. Other times, when

I expected him to get angry, he wouldn't. Like when the barn burned, I ran up the road to meet him coming home from work to make sure that he didn't blow up in the yard at my mom for 'whatever'. When I told him about the fire, he replied that there was nothing he could do it about it now. I was shocked that he just brushed it off and when we got in the yard, he was concerned about the safety of all of us and the animals. He was very calm. Not the reaction that any of us had expected but was a welcomed one.

At six years old, old enough to start school, I wasn't allowed to because we were French. I didn't understand. Our landlord went to bat for us. He was paying taxes to two schools. He figured that owning two properties, one in each school district, I should be allowed in one of the schools—we lived about one and a half miles from both schools. It took him a year before he got results and finally, I was allowed to start school when I was seven years old. I was really anxious to go. My mom had me wanting to start school since she wasn't able to go to school because of her being too sick. She had explained that I would learn a lot of new stuff at school and that it would be fun. I wanted that. That love of school carried me through all my years in school and I continue to want to learn still to this day.

It was a long way to walk but I didn't have to do it alone. By then my brother Arthur, who was almost six years old, started school at the same time as I did. By the time we got to school in the wintertime, the stove had been lit and it was warming up in the school room. We would hang our outer clothing up near the stove to dry so they would be good to go by the time we were to walk back home. If the road was closed because of being snow covered, we still had to go to school because the teacher would also walk to school. There were no "snow days." I remember walking on the high snow banks to school and had to jump off when we got to the end of the road. I went to that one-room school for three years before we moved again.

By the time there were three of us going to school, we got to know the milk truck driver and hitched a ride with him to school. We knew we had to be on the road by the time he came by in order to be picked up. He was picking up the milk from across the road from us. He drove right by our school so it was perfect—until one morning it wasn't. He had a girl with him and he forgot to stop at the school to let us off. We were in the back of the truck with the milk cans. We banged on the front of the back of the truck to get his attention but he didn't hear us. We had to jump off with him going at full speed. We got to school on time, but we were so dusty from the long dusty grass that we jumped into. All roads around us were dirt roads in those days. After that, if he had his girlfriends with him, he didn't pick us up nor did we want to take the chance again. We only took the ride if we could ride in front with him.

The one-room school had a wood burning stove in the back, beside the door to warm up the room so we could learn. The front of the room had a blackboard from one wall to the other. Each section of that blackboard was used for each of the eight grades. There were between forty-three and forty-six kids with one teacher to teach eight subjects to each grade. That made a total of sixty-four subjects to teach in one day. Teachers had to love their jobs for sure back then.

We also walked to church most times. It was farther still than the school—at least twice as far. To prepare for our First Communion, and the following year, Confirmation, Arthur and I had to walk there on Saturdays for instructions from the priest and again with the family on Sundays. During the wintertime, we would usually go by horse and cart. I remember all those prayers we had to memorize so we could be ready and be accepted to do our Communion and Confirmation. The problem at the time, we didn't know what the English words of the prayers meant. No one explained them to us. I wonder, did *they* even know what they meant? Maybe that is why they didn't explain them. I remember saying "Jesus" in the prayer and would shrink back or laugh because I had only heard it in cursing. It was one of the first English words I learned and was told that it was swearing. It was a long time before I was comfortable with the word and to understand it was God. It took a while longer to learn He is the Son of God.

The night Dad came home with his first car, a Model "A", Mom woke us up and we all were allowed to go outside and see it. What a celebration time! Dad gave us a ride. We were one of the last ones on our road to get a car. Now Dad could leave for work a little later and drive into the city to work instead of walking all the way. He also got home a little earlier. We got to see him a little more often. Going to church was also different. We all piled into the car and I felt we were rich going to church in a car instead of walking or by horse and cart. I did miss the horse-drawn sleigh though for Christmas Eve mass. We would all cuddle up with blankets in that sleigh and go to church on Christmas Eve with the snow coming down. To me that is the perfect Christmas Eve scenery.

One night Mom and Dad decided to take us to a movie. It was a drive-in. We all got to see it while we sat in the car. A small radio that was attached to a post was put on our car window and the movie could be heard that way. I don't remember the movie but I do remember two guys in it were called Andre and Pierre and I thought they were really good looking. I do remember something about them being identical twins not living near each other. The only other movie I remember Mom and Dad taking us to is a movie theatre in a nearby town when we were in our early teens. The name of the movie was *Mom and Dad*. It was an educational film about women and men with sexually transmitted diseases and venereal disease and it showed graphic pictures of the disease. Arthur and I didn't sit with Mom and Dad in the theatre. We figured it was Mom and Dad's way of educating us about what could happen if you had sex.

Another time Mom told me of a test that was done on her when she was doing housework for someone else. The lady had put money on her dresser to see if Mom would steal it when she was cleaning in the bedroom. She didn't. Mom and I visited our landlady one day and as I was looking around, I went into the daughter's bedroom. Lo and behold! I saw some change on her bedroom dresser. She was not at home. I thought of what Mom had told me and I didn't touch it. Later I found out that it would have been stealing. I was still learning what was right and wrong. I could say that I never forgot this and never took anything that wasn't mine; but sadly, this is not so. You will read about it later.

Another time I was doing housework for a lady in the village. I had to dust off the dresser in the master bedroom. There was money in a bowl on the dresser. The story came to my mind again. I told the lady I was working for that there was money on her dresser. She said she was not testing me and forgotten it on the dresser that morning.

After I started school, on Sunday nights I was allowed to go with my girlfriend, who was much older than I, to a neighbour's place, to watch TV. By this time electricity started to come to homes near us. We didn't call it a TV though. We called it a 'picture radio' because it was like a radio but you could see the picture. This neighbour was the first to get a TV for miles around. We watched *Father knows Best* and *Ed Sullivan Show*. One night, some of my comic book heroes, Roy Rogers and Dale Evans, were on TV. We were allowed to stay and watch it. I had to be home by a certain time because of school the next day though.

I started collecting stamps from all over the world at about nine years old. I joined a club that were selling stamps and with any of the little money I could get I spent it on my collection. Mom paid for some as well. I continued to collect stamps until after I was married and had children. By then, I had quite a collection. One night I noticed that the girls had gotten into my collection and had ripped a few of them up. I gave up the collection and knowing that our nephew collected stamps I gave him the whole collection and anything that went with it. I never collected them again. That was the beginning of collecting things, stones, books, old coins, hockey cards, whatever I decided at the time.

The summer I passed into grade four we had to move again. The landlord's son was getting married and he needed the house. We hated to move and the landlord felt bad that he had to tell us to move out but that was why he had kept it in the first place.

This time, we moved to a large old run-down house way out in the field. It was owned by one of my parents' friends. It was to be temporary. The morning after we moved, we woke up to see a cow looking in on us through the crack in the bottom of the back door. We were sleeping on the floor; we hadn't made up the beds yet. For the few months we lived there, we had fun. There was an upstairs that was empty and we used it to play hide and go seek if it was raining outside. Being in the woods, there was plenty of space outside to play as well.

It was late in September and the landlord said it was time for us to go to school. He was one of the trustees of that school. That first day, my brothers Arthur, Oscar and Sister Anna and I walked to school but when we got there, the teacher asked what we were doing there. I said, "Coming to school." She told us that no, we were not, and to go back home. So, we did.

Half way home the landlord came by and asked us why we were not in school. I told him what had happened. He told us to go home and that is where we stayed until late October before the landlord could get us into the school. This time it wasn't because we were French. The landlord was French. The teacher didn't want any more students to teach. The day we did go back to school the teacher said she wouldn't teach us. Being very stubborn, that day I made up my mind that she could not fail me and I would learn on my own and follow as she taught the others. I was in grade 4 and only ten years old at the time. And that is what I did.

It was getting too cold in the house we were in so we moved again. This time closer to the school to a house on a hill that had electricity. We had had no such thing before and I took pleasure in switching the lights on and off until my mother told me to quit it. She had to tell me many times because I liked to see the lights going on and off. It was new to me. Kids would come from all around to slide down our hill. This place had lots of apple trees—we saved some wrapped in newspaper, in the cellar for the winter. Also, everywhere we went there were a lot of snakes. You couldn't stand still for a few seconds before there would be one sliding up your leg. Had that happen once as my mom tried to tell me that it was happening but she wasn't fast enough. I just reached down and took it off. Snakes didn't bother me at that time.

The kids here bullied us and beat us up on the way to and from school so after a while we started to walk through the fields and the bush to get to school. We were late every morning but at least we didn't get beaten up. We never told my mom or the teacher. Mom would have gone to the trustees and the teacher didn't care anyways. We knew if we told, things would be worse. One of the girls who was the ringleader was the daughter of the trustee and she thought she was better than us because we were renters not owners of a farm like she was.

After school I was allowed to go to a friend's place, next door, to watch TV for about an hour before going home. That is where I first watched *Howdy Doody* and *Long John Silver*.

I had the mumps on both side of my face at the same time. I thought I looked like a chipmunk with their cheeks full of food, but I wasn't sick so I continued going to school every day hoping that the teacher would get it and miss school but she didn't. I didn't need her anyways; she wasn't teaching me as she had said she wouldn't. I didn't know at the time that she had had the mumps and she wouldn't get it again.

We owned a colt and the next-door neighbour owned a heifer. The colt would jump the fence and go over to the neighbours and the calf would come to our place. Just before Christmas that year Dad and our neighbour decided to switch. Solved the problem. We got the best part, I think. The heifer was 'with calf', and on Christmas Eve she gave birth. That cow and her calf was the start of our herd we later had on the farm.

Chapter 4

Dad is so Happy

Mom and Dad bought a farm for $1500 and so we moved there in the spring before the end of the school year. We moved almost across the road from the school I started in. I passed my grade that year because I had kept the promise I had made to myself, to pass even though the previous teacher didn't teach me. I later learned that she didn't even have a licence to teach and was let go.

Being used to having electricity by this time my dad had Mom's brother-in-law, who was an electrician, put in the electricity in the house. The house had been used as a shooting target for years by the boys in the community. Mom took out all the lead and filled all the holes left by the bullets that had been shot into the house. Then she painted the walls in the summer kitchen and wallpapered the other rooms. This house had a summer kitchen, a winter kitchen, a parlour and an upstairs with a large room, two separate bedrooms and an attic all on the same floor. It was a real fix-it-upper. There was no insulation in the house and only a cellar under the winter kitchen. An under the floor furnace was installed for heat but we still had a wood and coal stove in the winter kitchen. We also had a wood cook stove in the summer kitchen which was made an all-season kitchen after the insulation was put in.

Dad knocked down the parlour walls between it and the winter kitchen one Sunday afternoon and an archway was made. It became our living room. In the winter kitchen, a bedroom was built on one end and a large pantry closet was built on the opposite end. Later a toilet and drawers were built under the stairs on the opposite wall from the closet. By then we were using the summer kitchen year round and no longer needed a winter kitchen. Dad figured we could use a living room instead of a parlour that only visitors were allowed. Everyone was allowed in the living room. He said parlours were for rich people and we were not rich people.

Every fall Dad would embank the whole house to help keep out the cold. To embank meant to build a wood wall all around the house and then fill it with earth. In the spring he would take it all down until the fall and build it up again. One year Mom decided to make a flower bed in the embankment and Dad did not have to do all that work every spring and fall again. It made our yard a lot prettier.

We painted the wood kitchen floor every year to keep it looking good. That was one of the first jobs Archie had to do when I started going out with him. His second was to help rebuild the barn after the old one burned down.

Having the cow and her calf from the last place we lived in, we started to milk them and started our small herd from them. Besides the cows, we had two horses. Every year we would buy and raise pigs, ducks, chickens, and geese to kill for food for the winter. We had turkeys for a few years only. I understood at the time that they were too much work or something like that. Also, for a few years we raised rabbits to eat. Mom wanted goat's milk so she got a goat one summer.

I would sometimes find a chipmunk or a bird that I would nurse back to health. We had cats for the barn only. Dad didn't want cats in the house—they were to catch mice in the barn. We also had a dog most of the time. Someone gave me a kitten once but as I said Dad didn't want cats in the house so I wasn't allowed to keep it. He put it in a sack with rocks and took me down to the creek to show me what he does with kittens he didn't want. He threw it in the creek to drown it. I never had a kitten again.

The mare we had become lame and Dad decided to sell her. She was going to the glue factory, I was told. I had grown up with her and didn't want to see her go. The day the buyer was coming to pick her up and pay for her, Dad had to go somewhere else and wasn't home when he came. He wanted me to take the money and give him the mare. The man came with a $100 bill and didn't have any change. He wanted to take the mare and come back later to pay Dad. I wouldn't let him take her. He would have to come back. He did and Dad dealt with him. I made sure I wasn't around to see her go. Chance, the mare's name, had been the only pet that I had had since Rex was killed. To Dad's way of thinking, she wasn't any more use because she was lame, but to me, I still could ride her and play around her.

On summer Sunday afternoon's Dad would take us fishing until we had enough for the following Friday night's supper. Being Catholic we didn't eat meat on Fridays. Mom would keep them in a tub—to keep them alive—until it was time to kill them to eat. That way they were fresh. I don't remember what we ate in the winter if not meat. The beef and pork were preserved in salt. After my mom bought our first freezer all the meat was stored in that.

She saved family allowance money and sold her hand crochet doilies to buy what she needed. We also had 100 quarts of raspberries, 100 quarts of strawberries, peaches, blueberries, blackberries and all kinds of pickles and corn relish in jars and crocks. We also had brought in a large bin full of potatoes, carrots, beets, turnips, and onions. We wrapped apples individually in newspaper and put them in the cellar. This was all done to prepare for the winter to last until the next summer.

The picking of weeds in the large garden was part of our job with Mom. The vegetables we grew were to feed us all year round and some for seed for the next year. The garden had to yield a good crop if we didn't want to go hungry. I remember for the first few years that we lived on the farm, we had to pull up wild mustard plants and not leave any in the field. We had to do this until there were no mustard plants growing on our farm. It took a year or two to get rid of all the mustard plants. This meant that we had to make sure that every plant did not reseed the soil. Putting all the plants in a large pile we would have to burn them and not leave them to reseed. One year, the whole field caught on fire but we were able to stop it from spreading into another field or the buildings. When the grass regrew, it was greener and cleaned from all the weeds. The next year that field became a bigger vegetable garden.

The bread truck would come every Monday, Wednesday, and Friday and we would get twenty loaves of bread each trip he made. With all the school lunches and breakfast or all the times we wanted a sandwich, we really needed to get more than twenty. Mom would only have enough money to buy twenty loaves and sometimes had to put it on credit. If she did have extra, sometimes she would treat us with a cake she didn't bake.

We planted corn by the field not by the few rows like everyone else. When it was ready to pick, we would pick a few dozen at a time. We set up a table at the road and yelled at cars as they drove by, "Corn for sale!" Cars didn't drive as fast in those days and we were on a dirt road. We sold a farmer's dozen (thirteen) for 50 cents. We had repeat buyers as each summer went by. With the money we made —all given to Dad—was separated among each of us to pay for our trip to the city exhibition. That was our reward for all the work we did throughout the year. After we had picked the 100 quarts of raspberries and 100 quarts of strawberries, we were allowed to sell them and add that money to the pot. Raspberries were easier because we didn't have to bend down to pick them. Remember, I am talking about wild berries, not the big tame ones we have today.

I was so naive. One day I saw Mom and Dad walking back from the bush and Dad was so happy. It seemed that he was never happy and now he was happy? I just wanted to know how to make him happy. So, I said to Mom, "Mom whatever you did when you were in the bush can you do it again? Dad is so happy!" Thinking back now I wonder what Mom might have thought when I asked that dumb question. Today, I know what they did. With all the kids at home, they did what they couldn't do at home. There was no privacy.

Mom would tell us not to go around without something on our feet. I always wore shoes and socks in the summertime. There was some sort of construction at the back of the house on the way to the outhouse. Boards with nails sticking up and other debris that was dangerous without shoes. One day I was running, and ran through the site with the boards and nails. I only got half way through when I stepped on a nail and it went right through my shoe, sock and my foot. Since the board was too large for me to carry it, with it on my foot, I either had to wait until someone saw me and could get Mom to come, or I had to pull my own foot off the nail. Not wanting to prolong the pain, I yanked it off the nail, and went into the house leaving a trail of blood. Mom made a hot poultice with hot milk and bread and put it on. It was really hot but Mom said that it had to be hot to draw the poison of the rusty nail out. When it was cool, another one was put on. I had to walk around for a few days with mushy bread and milk in my socks and shoe. Mom wanted to be sure that there was no infection to set in. Dad cleaned up the boards.

We would target practice with Dad's army rifle—a 22cal. Mom got so good at it she was able to shoot a groundhog a field away. In the summer, that was some of our meat. In November, Dad would kill a pig and Mom would kill the chickens, geese and ducks, keeping enough hens for eggs to eat all winter. While Dad held the dying pig Mom and I would hold a pot under the flowing blood to save to make blood pudding. We had to make sure that the blood didn't get dirty. In the spring we would start the stock over again by buying chicks, and whatever we needed to raise for food. Of course, having all these animals, someone had to feed and take care of them. That fell on Mom and us kids. Dad was always at work except on weekends. Sunday was a day for church and then rest with no work except feed the animals and milk the cows. No field work was done on Sunday.

The next-door neighbours had a television and we wanted to see the shows at 10:00 Saturday mornings but we had to have our own work done at home and the friends next door had to have theirs done before we could watch it. The program was "Cowboy Corner" and every Saturday there would be a different cowboy on it. Cowboys like Gene Autry, Roy Rogers and Dale Evans, Wild Bill Hickok, Annie Oakley, and many more. If we didn't have our work done yet and our friends had theirs done first, they would come over and help us. If we were done first, we would go help them. Sometimes, if we had nothing else to do that day, instead of going out to play, we would watch a movie after the cowboy show.

One Saturday, we got watching a war movie and didn't hear Mr. Thompson come home. We knew not to be watching anything with war or guns or anything to do with violence. We never got to watch the end of the movie. Mrs. Thompson came in the room, shut off the TV and told us to go home. She was nice about it but we knew we had all messed up. As we were passing through the kitchen to go out of the house, we saw Mr. Thompson crouched in the corner under the kitchen table. He was shaking and had his hands over his head and his head between his knees. Mrs. Thompson was trying to calm him down and get him to come out from under the table. We knew why he was under that table. We really felt bad for what we had done to him. After that we watched the cowboy movies and then would shut the TV off not taking a chance in doing that to him again. We knew he would be home for lunchtime so we were safe to watch "Cowboy Corner" but nothing else. We still listened to make sure he didn't come home early and get caught watching westerns. It was the shooting in the shows that set him off.

He had been in the Second World War and in one of the battles, he had been left for dead with the rest of his platoon in an open field. He lay there for days before someone found him with a bayonet through his body. He had been so traumatized that he was sent home after he healed. He was left with fragments of the bayonet in his body and was deaf the rest of his life. Today there are treatments for PTSD but there was nothing back then.

My brothers and I had to hand milk the cows every morning and night. We got up at 4:30 to get the cows in from the field, milk them, and then get ready for school. Dad was at work and Mom's hands were too weak to do the milking. When Dad bought an electric milking machine, I truly resented it. I was being replace by a stupid machine. Not taking into consideration that the machine had to be attached to the udders and then taken off again never entered my mind. I told Dad that I wouldn't do it any longer that if he wanted a machine to do the milking then I wasn't even going to the barn to help. And I didn't. By then, I was finished school.

I preferred to be out in the fields and outside to do the work instead of housework. I hated housework. My brother Arthur preferred to be in the house doing the housework. Except on threshing days, he had to be out in the field with the men, and I had to be in the house when they came in to eat. While they were in the field, I was in the granary with Dad emptying the grain from the bags into the granary and then had to go in and help Mom serve the meals.

I was treated as a boy by my dad because when I was born, he had wanted a boy. It got to be that I *wanted* to be a boy, especially when I matured. It was not fun to be a girl and mature when you're barely nine years old. I really hated it and remember the day my girlfriend, who liked being a girl, was taken for a boy and I was taken for a girl by someone who was driving by and stopped to ask for directions. We were both offended. She had a bra on that she had stuffed to try to make her look like she had a large breast and I had mine strapped down to try to look flat like a boy but neither of us succeeded in fooling anyone. By the time I was twelve years old, I was wearing a 36C bra.

Loving to read, I started to read books that I got from the library in the village. It was opened every two weeks and could only get so many books at a time. The librarian let me have more books because she would test me to see if I really was reading the books I had brought home and found that I did indeed read them. I was allowed twice as many. I read every one of them before the next two weeks. I read every Nancy Drew, Hardy Boys, Bobbsey Twins, Trixie Belden—a few I don't remember the names of now—I could get my hands on. I think this is why I wanted to be a private detective when I grew up. I used to dream of being one. That was besides wanting to become a teacher.

The community garbage dump was only one mile away, just at the edge of our farm. We would go often to see what we could find. That is where I obtained a lot of my first library of books. One day Arthur went to the dump and came back and told me that there were boxes of books there that had just been dropped off. I went, picked out what I wanted and got about three boxes of books to bring home. I didn't want anyone to see me go home with them so I came home through the fields, going back and forth bringing the boxes until I got home. I felt I was very fortunate to get all those books. Besides I had no money to buy books and these were free. More about my books later. I still have the poetry books that I got that day. I love poetry.

My brother Andre was born but I don't remember the events around it. Not sure if he was born at home or in the hospital. When he was two years old, he became paralyzed and was diagnosed with Paralyzes pneumonia Polio and lived in the hospital in the city for another three years. He eventually was able to walk, with braces and then without. Today they don't know if he actually had polio or not but he was completely paralyzed.

When I was eleven years old my mother became pregnant again and was very ill. She became bedridden so I missed eight months of the ten months of the school year to stay home with her, so my father could go to work. I also had my brother William and sister Pauline at home to look after. My baby sister Rebecca was born at home, but her twin was still-born. The doctor was so sick that he didn't realize that she was too small and should have been in a hospital incubator. My father had to help him down the stairs he was that weak after the baby was born. I was able to hold my sister in one hand she was so small.

At about three weeks, the next-door neighbour, who was a nurse, came over to see how things were and noticed that the baby wasn't doing so well. My sister was taken to the hospital to be put in an incubator until she was heavy enough to come back home. I still had to stay home with Mom and the kids. By the time Dad came home, I went from being a caretaker to a child again. I had done OK all day but by the time Dad came home I had had enough and I reverted back to being a child of eleven years old.

One afternoon I was upstairs with Mom and the baby and my brother and sister were downstairs. Pauline yelled up the stairs, "William has a bond fire on the floor." I rushed down the stairs and Mom yelled to me, "Burn his hands in the fire." She couldn't move out of bed and was scared that she would burn in it. Not thinking otherwise and obeying what Mom said to do when I got downstairs, I put the fire out and then grabbed him and held both his hand on the hot coals in the buck stove. After that I went back upstairs to look after Mom and the baby. William went outside to wait for Dad.

When Dad came home and saw what I did to William he came in the house and asked what happened. I pointed to the burn mark on the floor and told him what happened. For some reason Dad never scolded me or yelled at me. He took care of the burns on my brother's hands. My brother never forgot that day and never played with fire when I was around. Unfortunately, he still loved to play with fire but just didn't do it when I was around.

The whole eight months I was still doing my school work as the teacher would stop in after school, give me my assignment for the next day, take that day's work to correct it and when exams time came, I was allowed to go to school to write them. Arthur, who was in the same grade as I, would come home one way and I was allowed to go, but had to take another way to the school. One of us would take the road and the other would go through the field. That way he couldn't tell me any of the questions ahead of time. I passed that year in school, thanks to my teacher and my love of school. I also believe it was my love of reading that helped me. Two other brothers, Andre and Jimmy, were also born while we were living in the farm house. I now had five brothers and three sisters. My mother had lost one—it was a boy—he was born in the hospital and buried before my mother came home. My mother wanted twelve children and she had eleven. The doctor wouldn't let her try for the twelfth. He said she wasn't strong enough to get through the next pregnancy.

Later in life, my mother and I talked about that time in our lives. She apologized saying, that I should never have been put in that position and all the responsibilities I had to shoulder. I had never given it a second thought, that's the way it was. I didn't know any different. My mother had felt guilty the whole time. Hopefully by talking about it, it relieved some of the guilt.

Chapter 5
MARIJUANA FLOWER

Being out of school for that many months started the women of our church to gossip and they figured they knew why I was out of school that long. When a baby emerged, they figured it was mine. We had no idea this was all happening until one day Archie and I were volunteering at a dinner that the church had given and one of the women asked me how my oldest daughter was. Thinking she meant Annette, I told her that she was in British Columbia and going to school there.

The woman said, "No, not Annette, *your* oldest daughter."

I said, "Annette is my oldest daughter."

Another woman then came in on the conversation and said, "She means Rebecca."

I looked at them strangely and wandered what in the world they were talking about. They then told me about when I was off school that winter for so long when Rebecca was born. Wasn't she mine? I was shocked and insulted. How could they think that way? I straightened them out and told them that I was only eleven years old and NO! Rebecca was not mine but she was my sister. End of conversation. These women were supposed to be Christian women and they were judging me and my mom? They had been gossiping about me for twenty-seven years and we never knew it.

One winter's day, another time Mom was sick in bed, I was looking after her in her makeshift downstairs bedroom in the living room. Something was going on in the kitchen. Dad walked in on it and then came into Mom's bedroom and started yelling at her and blaming her for whatever was happening in the kitchen. She was unable to get out of bed. I listened to it at first, but then I just yelled at Dad, "Shut up!" What a big mistake! I knew not to talk back to them. He turned to me and said, "Get out of the house." I went upstairs, got some things, like a book, went out to the hay-loft and stayed there for the rest of the day.

There was a small hole in the barn wall of the hayloft and I could see out. After a few hours, I watched Dad looking for me and he looked worried that I wasn't around. I didn't go out then, I thought, *Good, now he will know he did wrong for yelling at Mom.* It was cold outside but not in the hayloft. When it started to get dark, I sneaked into the house. I did let Mom know that I was back before going to my bedroom. I thought that day that it was my responsibility to take care of whatever happened in the kitchen, not my mother. I could have told my father that but figured he should have known it. If he had yelled at me then he wouldn't be wrong in yelling. Now that I'm older I know that Dad was probably blaming himself because he was outside instead of being in the house looking after things.

There was a very large picture of the Sacred Heart of Jesus hanging on the wall in the summer kitchen. One day Arthur and I got into a discussion about Jesus being able to see us everywhere and always. There was a door into the main part of the house, living room on one side of that wall and a door to go outside on the other. One of us stood at the door to go outside and the other one at the door to go into the living room.

I said, "He's looking at me," meaning Jesus was looking at me.

Arthur said, "No, He's looking at me."

We changed places and found that Jesus was looking at both of us at the same time. Mom had always told us that Jesus could see us wherever we were, and that we could never hide from Him. That day confirmed to us that she was right. God could see each one of us no matter where we were. When I started reading the Bible, I found it in the Bible.

(*Jeremiah 23:24: Who can hide in secret places so that I cannot see them?" declares the Lord. "Do not I fill heaven and earth?" declares the Lord.*) Today I believe that He is always with me, that I am never alone. He is my constant companion.

In the wintertime, we played in the snow, building forts, walking on the high snow banks along the roads and we would play hockey out in the field when the ice would form on the frozen field. We took dried-out and frozen cow poop as pucks and any stick that was straight or almost straight and strong enough to use as a hockey stick. If it broke, we would just find another stick to use. I remember playing until it got dark or until Mom would call us in to go to bed.

In the summer, we played Cowboys and Indians, hide and seek, skipping rope, anti-I-over, baseball and would make up our own games by seeing who could do something better than the other, like lifting a solid large metal object off the ground, or who could bend over backwards over a chair. I would do a lot of reading, and play with my paper dolls. When we got old enough, Mom let us go to the swimming hole in an old gravel pit across the road from the dump one mile away. We spent a lot of time there, especially on hot days. There I learned to swim until one day, just fooling around in the water, a friend brought me in the middle and dropped me. We were not aware that the middle was dangerous. We had never gone down deep enough. There was a whirlpool in the bottom that pulled me down and I panicked. No matter what I did, it was sucking me down into it. I surfaced but couldn't stay on top. I was going down for the third time by the time the others noticed that I was in trouble. The guy who dropped me in the middle was the one who came in and saved me. Everyone stayed away from the middle of that swimming hole after that. I became afraid of water after that and wasn't able to let myself go to swim again. This affected me throughout the rest of my life.

There was no TV to keep us in the house so we were outside all day. We didn't need to go in the house except to eat or go to bed. Mom knew where we were at all times. Somewhere on the farm of 161 acres. We would let her know if we went elsewhere. If she needed us to come to the house she would blow the car horn once, if for supper it would be twice.

An extra-long blast of the horn was never discussed, but when it did happen, one Sunday afternoon, we knew it was an emergency. We ran all the way home—we were at the end of the property about a mile away. Got home to find that Dad had cut off his finger working on his car. He never worked on Sunday again, especially on his car. He said that God had punished him for not respecting the Lords Day of rest. We knew then what Sunday was for, besides going to church. We also were told that if we did wrong things God would punish us. The doctors were not able to put it back on so Dad had Mom put it in alcohol in a bottle to preserve it so that when he died, we could put it in the coffin with him. He always said that he didn't want to meet Jesus with his body incomplete. It became an object of interest to show all our friends. Some of them thought that it was weird but we took it as normal. Good thing there was no show and tell in the school then or one of us might have brought it to show and tell. We did put it in Dad's pocket of his jacket in the coffin with him before he was buried.

I later learned in life that God is not a punishing God but He is a loving God. This makes such a big difference in my life. Anyone who has been told that. It is a lie. God does not punish us; he does admonish us for our wrongs but He knows we are only human and we make mistakes. He forgives us and loves us unconditionally. He does not like what we do, but He loves us.

Some other fun we had when we were growing up were contests. Mom, Arthur and I trying to finish first in splitting wood and stacking it into cords making it play instead of work. Mom who was almost nine months pregnant at the time always won. She never let us win. From that, I learned that if I wanted something I would have to work for it and not expect it to come to me freely. Mom told us that if Dad ever asked who did the wood, I was to say Arthur and I did it, omitting that my mom also did as much. Later in life I asked and she said, "He never did ask, did he?" It probably never occurred to him that she would have done it because of her pregnancy. He believed if a woman was pregnant, she wasn't to do anything. I found that out when I was pregnant with my second child and living back at home.

When I was fifteen years old, in 1960, I put an ad in the "Family Herald" a farm newspaper out of Western Canada. There was a column with letters asking for pen pals. I sent in a letter to be put in that column. I received about 100 letters, and answered them all.

Would be female private eye

What do you think of a girl wanting to be a private eye? I hope to be one some day.

My favorite singers are Fabian, Johnny Horton, Johnny Cash, Elvis Presley and others.

I would like the words to Sink The Bismark, Billy The Kid and El Paso.

I am a 5'2" dark-eyed brunette who was 15 July 22. I start high school in the fall. Please write.

RITA
R.R.4, Osgoode, Ont.

Some, I got letters back, others not. I did have about twenty-five continuous pen pals until I was married. Letters in those days were only a few cents for a stamp. I started selling food flavourings to make the money to buy the envelopes and stamps. My pen pals were from coast to coast in Canada. I have been selling something ever since then.

I inherited my dad's problem, as most of my brothers and sisters did, of wetting the bed. Mom would wake us up before she went to bed to have us go to the toilet but it just didn't seem to help. We didn't have anything to drink after supper either. I was in my early teens before I didn't wet my bed every night. After that I would usually wake up with my bed wet on the first night of my period. That went on until I was about eighteen years old. No matter what I tried nothing seemed to help.

I had a sore throat a lot and went to the doctor and was told that I would have to have my tonsils out. I was fifteen years old and he said I should have had them out at an earlier age and it would be harder on me. I had them taken out and remember having only jello and ice cream to eat for a few days. I couldn't eat anything hot. I had a gauze stuffing in my throat so I wouldn't bleed. I was to breathe only from my nose. While I was in the hospital I asked if they could find out why I was wetting the bed. They sent me back into the operating room, asleep, and ran some sort of test on my kidneys but found nothing. They didn't check my bladder.

When in high school, in the evenings I would get severe pain in my left side. This happened over and over again until Mom took me to the doctor for it. I was in the doctor's office in the day time, when I never had the pain. The doctor said it was my appendix and he would have to wait until they burst before he could operate on them. A few years later, I was watching a movie and in it was a person who had a burst appendix and almost died because the appendix poisoned the body. I realized then that if my appendix *had* burst, I could be dead. I never trusted that doctor again.

After we got a B&W TV set—that's all there was those days—on Friday nights one of the new neighbours would come over to watch hockey and we would sit and drink coffee while watching TV. One week we ran out of coffee and all week my mom, brother Arthur and I had a headache and couldn't find any reason for it. Friday evening was shopping time. My dad would get paid then and that was when the trip into the village was done to get food. After putting the food away, we all sat down and had a cup of instant coffee—that is what we used—we noticed that our headaches were gone. We had become addicted. I slowed down the drinking of coffee after that, until after I was married. I drank tea instead.

I learned respect for my elders by not using their first names. We would have to call them by Mr., Mrs., Aunt, Uncle, or Sir and Madame. Work ethics I learned by working alongside my dad out in the field, granary, and Mom in the house and outside. I also learned not to lie. We couldn't get away with it even if we did try. I did forget and tried a few times. Mom could read our minds. She also could read tea leaves. I once ask her why she wasn't charging people and make money doing it. Her reply was, "God didn't give me the gift to make money from it." She used it to help raise us. After all, she did have nine kids to keep in line. Not an easy task at times. She asked God after we were all grown up to take the gift away because it was causing her too much pain. She knew what we were all thinking and when my sister Anna lied and was mean to her, my mother couldn't take it. Also, she had a lot of trouble with two of my brothers, Oscar and William. God did as she asked and she no longer could read us. By this time, we had families of our own and my mom did not need the gift any longer to cope. By then, we had all learned that we were to always tell the truth no matter what.

Our kitchen table broke. Dad got a full sheet of heavy plywood and used the table legs to put the plywood on top to make our table. He also made a long bench the full length of the table for us to sit on to eat. We could fit more people at the table. There were eleven of us to fit at that table and when our family started expanding, we needed another table as well. The second table was always needed at Christmas and New Year's time. The adults would be at the large table and the kids at the second table so we could all eat together. By the time Mom sold the farm there were about thirty-eight in the family besides some friends and relations also for the meal.

One Saturday morning, I woke up to find that Dad had Mom go sit on the field mower to cut down the hay. I was the one that usually was on the mower. Mom wasn't feeling well and should not have been out on the mower. The mower bounced you around so much that it was hard to hang on sometimes. You had to be alert to be able to raise the blade on time if there was something in the way that it might hit and break it. I was so angry that I thought, "I'll show him." I started up the half ton truck, that Dad had been using on the farm, and drove it out into the hay field, where the bails were ready to bring into the barn. Not knowing how to drive the half ton truck, I put it what I thought was in low gear and let it run on its own along the rows of bails as I was loading and stacking onto the back of it. Every now and then, I would steer it to go in the right direction. When the back was full, I drove it to the barn. The field was on the other side of the house and I had to drive on the road about 1000 yards, go through a deep ditch to go to the barnyard, and then to the barn. I then used the hay lift to get them into the hayloft. I was on my third load by the time Mom and Dad came back to the barn. All Dad told Mom was, "At least she could have put it in first gear instead of second to go through the ditch." The bails had jumped up and came back down, according to my mother's account of what she saw. I had driven the tractor many times so presumed that the gears were the same. Dad didn't let me go out again to bring in the rest of the bails from that field. He sent my two brothers, Arthur and Oscar. Dad had shown them how to drive it. The truck never left the field that day. Oscar, who was driving, had stripped the gears.

Because we were French, we were still having problems in the community. The village teens would call us names, beat us up, and one day when Mom and I were driving through the village they formed a line across the road to make us stop. I knew they planned on beating us up. This was the first time for Mom to be involved so she didn't know what they were doing. She slowed down and I told her not to stop. She was afraid to hit them with the car if they didn't move. We were close to a stop.

I yelled, "Step on it!"

She said, "I'm going to hit them!"

I said, "But they will beat us up, step on it."

She did but nipped one of them as they tried to get out of the way just in time. They never tried that again. My mom found it hard to believe that they would do what they did. She knew some of their parents, at least their mothers. Since we couldn't speak French while outside of the home and having to learn English, I lost most of my French language. Prejudice is not a good thing. I learned early in life.

One time, one of our policemen came to the house after another problem. He noticed a flower in Mom's flower bed in the embankment to the house and said, "Nice Marijuana flower."

"Oh!" I said, "Is that what it's called?" We had been given the flower but hadn't been told the name of it. The policeman realized that we didn't know it was a marijuana plant so he didn't say anything. It was years before we realized that it was illegal. It grew every year in that flower bed and added to the beauty of the bed. That policeman could have been mean and made us take it out or even charged us. He was to see that flower many times after that day but never said anything about it again.

I started high school when I was fifteen and really felt out of place. Going from a one-room school and eight grades to a ten-room school was almost too much for me. There were as many students in one class as there had been in the whole school where I had been. I still liked school but really had to study to keep up my grades. I also took a bus for the first time because the school was not within walking distance. To pay for my school supplies, like pens, pencil, writing books, text books, and whatever, I got a job of housecleaning every second Saturday for half a day.

I would get paid $4.40 every two weeks. I also babysat and sold garden seeds and food flavourings. I passed every grade until grade 12. I failed my grade 12.

This was because of the barn burning down and being the oldest I was depended on to stay up at night and watch that the fire didn't restart. There was no fire department in the village, only volunteers who were not trained to really do the work that needed to be done to put out a barn fire. I fell asleep during two of my exams. The teacher said that if I had done one more question on each one, she could have passed me, but because I didn't have enough done, she had to fail my grade. I repeated my grade 12 and passed. I graduated. That was in 1965.

Chapter 6

Fire

The summer between grade 11 and grade 12 I got a job travelling across the country selling magazines door to door. I got $2.00 per day and commission on whatever I sold. Unfortunately, I didn't sell much. Being only seventeen years old, I didn't know much yet about life and that I would have to lie to the people and tell them anything so they would buy from me. I found that telling them the truth that I was working to help me through high school didn't sell magazines. I did sell some one day but when I went to the restaurant to have my supper it was stolen out of my motel room. There was nothing anyone did about it. I was out of that money. The whole summer we stayed in motel rooms or hotel rooms. I did get out as far as Alberta and back but mostly I saw closed and slammed doors as I went to the houses. We didn't stay very long in any one place to have time to really see the towns we were in.

One day, I was out in the country and the houses were very far apart. I was dropped off at the end of the road and told that I would be picked up at a certain time at the other end. I was to go to each house in between. There weren't many but one of the houses I did stay longer than I was allowed to by the rules. The woman saw me coming up the road and got me in the house quickly. She wanted to know what I was doing in the country all by myself and told me that it was dangerous out there. It was cougar country and rattlesnake country. I hadn't seen any. I tried to tell her that I wasn't allowed to go into a house and when she insisted that I have something to eat, again I wasn't allowed to do it, I told her so. Her husband joined her in insisting that I eat before I was to go. Knowing that I didn't have much money to eat in the restaurant I sat down and ate. I did make it to the end of the road just in time to be picked up.

I had left home with $20 that Mom gave me, just in case, and came home at the end of the summer with less than that. I returned to finish my high school. I had to buy used text books because I didn't have the money to buy new ones. The next summer I didn't return to that job.

When I was in high school one summer, a gravel company was looking to buy gravel and they found some on our farm. At one point Dad thought that the company was cheating him on the amount of gravel being taken out and not getting paid for it. He asked me to stay and watch at the scales to make sure it wasn't happening. I got to know some of the men who were driving the dump trucks. One of them, Dick, asked me if I would go out with him and he also asked my parents. They said OK and I did. After a few times he brought one of his friends, Arnold, who I also got to know, from the gravel pit. We all went to my friend's house and something was needed from the store. My sister went with us because Arnold came as well. We bought what was needed and when we got back my sister and Dick, went into the house. Arnold asked me if I wanted to go for a ride because he wanted to talk to me and I said yes. Now thinking back, it was not the thing to do but I did. We went to the Light House where there was a dance going on and we sat in the car to talk. He told me not to get serious about Dick and asked if he had kissed me. When I said yes, he had, he continued the questioning.

He wanted to know if I felt anything when Dick kissed me. He asked if he could kiss me to see if it was the same as when Dick kissed me. I was so naive that I really did not know what he was getting at. After a few kisses, I still did not feel anything. To me they were just kisses, nothing more. He wouldn't tell me why I wasn't to get serious about Dick. We went somewhere else and we talked for a long time. When we noticed the time, it was two in the morning, we headed for home.

When we drove in the driveway, we saw a police car and Dad ran to the car. He was yelling at me to get in the house and he had his arm raised as if he was going to hit me. The police asked him if he was going to hit me and he said no. Dad yelled at Arnold to get off his property and never come back. The policeman took me into a room in our house to question me. Now this is where my ignorance really showed up. The policeman asked me if Arnold had touched me. I said yes that he had put his arms around me. The poor policeman tried to explain what he meant but I just did not understand. He asked me if Arnold had kissed me and if he had touched me in any other way besides putting his arms around me. I told him yes to being kissed but when the question of touching me in any other way I just did not know what he was talking about. Finally, he must have figured that I had not been molested in any way because he left.

The first thing my mom said to me was, "Dick is married, and so is Arnold." I became so angry. This was all Dick's fault but Arnold was getting the blame. Dick was the one who should have told me that he was married instead of going out with me. He stayed overnight and the next morning I was to go with him to help explain it to his wife as to where he had been all night. My brother Arthur also came with us. I sat in the back seat. I refused to sit in the front seat with him. My brother sat in the front seat. Somehow according to everyone else Dick was the good guy in all this because he was the one to call the police when I didn't come home.

Dick's wife was pregnant and when we got to his house, he went in alone to explain and then Arthur and I had to go in to confirm what he had told her. She was out of cigarettes and had to go to the store to buy more. She asked if I wanted to go with her. I said yes. I didn't want to be wherever Dick was any longer than I had to be. On the way to the store, she asked me questions and I answered them truthfully. I saw it hurt her and felt sorry for her. We did a lot of talking in the car and she also knew that I didn't like what Dick had done by going out with me when he was married and expecting a baby.

They later moved in with us after the baby was born because he wasn't working and they couldn't afford the rent where they were living. I still did not talk much to Dick, but his wife and I became very good friends until they moved away and we never heard from them since. I saw Arnold once after that. He stopped by one afternoon, when he knew Dad would be at work and I went out to talk with him. He was no longer friends with Dick and had moved but wanted to see how I was. Mom also came out to talk to him and told him that she didn't blame him for what had happened.

Since grade 7 I had wanted to become a teacher. The teacher would have me help her teach. After I was done my school work, she had me take over grade 3 and/or grade 4 to help them read, and teach them math—I was good at reading and math. I loved it until I had problems with my brother Oscar, who was in grade 4. He wouldn't do what I said because I was his sister and not the teacher. I asked her to not teach grade 4 after that. She agreed. When I passed grade 12, I wanted to go to teacher's college but the school principal advised me not to even try for it so I didn't. Now I know if I had I could have made it, but hindsight is 20/20. The graduation ceremony was held in September of the next school year.

When Dad finally allowed me to date it was with someone, he liked and trusted. Someone I had known since I was about nine years old. I was in grade 11 by then. I went with him for about a year but ended it one cold winter night—I know because I had to walk home from the corner about 1/4 mile away. It had been another night he ordered food for me and after I ate it said I had to pay for it. He decided to go parking again and I didn't want another wresting match so I just "froze" on him when he put his groping arms around me. The only thing I said was, "I want to go home." Eventually he had enough and drove to the corner and stopped, told me to get out and take care of myself.

The next day he came over and tried to talk me into going out with him again and I wouldn't talk to him. He talked my parents to letting my sister go out with him but she wasn't old enough to go out without a chaperone, so I had to accompany them. This went on for a few times until I said I had had enough. I knew he was doing this just to have me with him. At one point in our going out, he had asked me to marry him but I would have to change my religion. That was not acceptable and when I told my mother about it, she understood and agreed. Dad never knew, as far as I know, that he had asked me to marry him.

When Arthur started dating, I went with his friend to make it a double date and that became a disaster as well. The guy drank and it got to the point that I gave him an ultimatum—the drink or me. He took the drink but thought he still could have me. I didn't know anything about alcoholics and their way of thinking back then. He became a problem after I met my future husband, Archie. He told Archie that he had planned on asking me to marry him, but he had never mentioned it to me. He seemed to be at a lot of the same parties we were at and he got drunk every time. When he was out of control, I was called upon to settle him down. Now I know that that was his way of getting me to pay attention to him. One night, again, I had had enough. When Archie came to get me to go settle him down, I said, no, I am not responsible for him and won't do it anymore. That was the end of that relationship.

The summer, 1965 is when I met my husband-to-be, Archie. I was home alone with my father—we didn't see eye to eye on anything—my mother, and siblings were all somewhere else. My girlfriend came over with her boyfriend and a guy and asked if I wanted to go to the movies with them, but as a date for the guy in the back seat.

I asked, "What's he like?" knowing she knew what I meant—I didn't want a wrestling match from trying to not be mauled.

She said, "He's not like that."

So, I said, "Does he have the money?"

She said yes. So, I said yes, I will go.

She knew about the one guy I went with who had made me pay my own way and I didn't have any money that day. He sat on one end of the seat and I sat on the other end and watched the movie. It took some time before we sat together in the middle. And the rest as they say is history. That was July and by the following July 1966 we were married. Years later Archie and I talked about that night and he told me that he heard the conversation through the open window. I had to explain to him what I meant about "What's he like?" and "Does he have the money?" Two of the things I never had a problem with when we went out together.

Right after I finished my grade 12 in June, I started work as a civil servant in the big city. Since I had no way into the city every day, I had to find a place to live closer to work. Archie found me a place. His former girlfriend was living in an apartment and I moved in with her. After a few months there was a problem and I found another place. A room in another apartment with someone else in a high-rise apartment until we were married. Moving into the city was a big change. I am a country girl and living in the city was hard for me. Having someone in the same building as me I found that privacy was gone and quietness was not to be expected. It is still like that today for me. In the country, I knew all the neighbours but, in the city, no one knew each other. I felt alone, lonely with no one to talk to after work until I went home on Friday night and spent the weekend at home with my family. I went back Sunday night to the apartment.

Archie left home and moved with my mom and dad while I lived in the city. He would borrow Dad's car to pick me up and bring me back home to the farmhouse. One night Dad's car wouldn't start so he borrowed a car from a friend of my family. This is the same man that I thought was my Uncle Tom until later. When we brought the car back, Tom said that it was for sale and if I gave him $100 it was mine. I thought he was kidding because it was April Fool's Day but the next day, he said he was serious. I didn't have a licence to drive but I bought it, put it and the insurance in Archie's name. Never thinking that he could have taken it and driven away and there was nothing I or anyone else could do about it. He never thought about it either.

My father did not want a toilet in the house, so there was no plumbing in the farmhouse until about 1965. He didn't want anyone to see him go into the toilet, he continued to go to the outhouse. It was built under the highest part of the bottom of the stairs. This was a back-in, walk-out toilet with a small sink only. Behind the rest of under the stairs, drawers were built to store things. Later, a bathtub was installed up in the attic of the house after it was transformed into bedrooms.

The day the barn burned down someone had to run to the next-door neighbour to make the call for the fire department. After that we got the telephone put in. It was a telephone with a crank that when we made a call, we would have to crank it to ring long or short rings. For instance, my aunt's ring was one long, five short and ours was one long, four short. We would have to count the rings when it rang so we knew who it was for. Sometimes, people would listen in on the party line so if you didn't want others to know something, you just didn't say it on the telephone. If the ring was an extra-long one, we knew it was a fire somewhere. If it rang, I would climb up on the very high windmill that we had to pump the water and look around for smoke. I could see for miles and usually knew about where the fire was. I wasn't afraid of heights then. I wouldn't do it now though.

From birth, I was afraid of sudden, loud noises, especially thunder. I don't really remember this but was told often by Mom that the teacher I had in grade 1 used to wear large flared skirts and when it thundered outside, she would have me get under her desk, cover the opening where she sat with her skirt. As she sat there, she would have all the school sing to the top of their voices until the thunder was over. She did this so I couldn't hear the loud thunder.

I do remember when I was pregnant the first time, Archie came home from work one day to find me hiding under the bed scared to death of the thunder. I have seen lightening split a tree in half and one set a barn (not ours) on fire. Today, I am not afraid of thunder or lightening. I know it is because I now know for a fact that God will protect me.

I would hold my breath going on a bridge over water. I was so terrified that when I was driving across a long one once, I held my breath and it took everything not to close my eyes. Archie, was in the car behind us and he called me on the citizen band radio (CB) to tell me to keep my eyes open. When we were off the bridge, he called me back and said, "You can breathe now." He knew that I had held my breath. I now can drive on a bridge because of my faith in God. Sometimes I have to really concentrate on God as I do because I can let the fear come back.

Chapter 7
Alcohol Poisoning

We got married when I was almost twenty-one years old. The night before the wedding at a gathering at my home I would empty Archie's beer, when others weren't watching, so he wouldn't get drunk. He agreed, but when they left, he went with his friends and got drunk. They brought him into his parents' house and left him on the floor in the living room. The next day—our wedding day—he had a hangover. The priest changed the time of the service and let me know but not Archie and my brother Arthur who were already in the church waiting an hour earlier. They waited two hours. Archie wanted to go out and have a cigarette but Arthur, who was best man, would not let him go out being afraid that he would not come back. I knew nothing about it until after we were married.

The meal was at the farm but the reception was in a hall. No alcohol was to be allowed in the hall. A lot of the people either spent most of the time outside or came in and out to get drinks. The toilets wouldn't flush. Later, after that night, talking with our friends, we found out that the tank was full of bottles of booze to keep cold. I had put mine behind the back seat of my father's car on the way to the hall but when I went out to get a drink it was gone. The only people who knew it was there were my father and father-in-law. No drinking that night. Also, every time Archie got one in his hand, someone would grab it out of his hand.

We left on our honeymoon in the $100 car I had bought, both of us without having had an alcoholic drink. The next morning, a knock on our motel room door woke us up. It was a little boy to tell us that our car had a flat tire. We had borrowed a spare tire before we left home and used that until we could replace it. I called my mom and asked if they were still planning on going to Upper Canada Village and she said yes. I told her where we were and they stopped in and we all spent the day together. That was our honeymoon. The next day was a work day.

The legal drinking age was twenty-one years old, and for my twenty-first birthday Archie and two of our friends took me to a bar to celebrate. Not knowing what to drink, he bought me rum and coke. Since he was driving, he didn't drink much—as far as I noticed anyway—but

I drank till he hardly had any of his paycheck left. He didn't make much money. On the way home I got hungry and asked to stop at the Dairy Queen. I got a banana split and just watching me eat it the two friends got sick. I wasn't feeling drunk at all. Every time I drank after that night, I would have something sweet afterwards. When I went home that weekend Mom got really worried. I was much like my grandfather and rum and coke was his drink. When he drank it, he would go back to being on the reservation and took the axe and wanted to scalp my grandmother. They had to lock him out of the house. My mom would tell us many times about it. She was afraid that it would affect me as it affected my grandfather. Alcohol didn't fizz on me much though. I could drink and drink and not feel drunk at all. I felt drunk only once or twice and my mood would get really bad because I was angry before I drank.

One New Year's Eve, I could have ended up with alcohol poisoning. We went to a New Year's Eve party with friends and drank all night. We did a lot of dancing and didn't notice how much I drank. I didn't feel anything. We had been invited to a house party as well so we left the hall party and went to our other friend's house party afterwards. As always it was 'bring you own booze' so I brought a 26 oz. bottle of rye. When we got there, she poured all of it in a very large glass and topped it up with a little bit of coke. She said that everyone had drank all they brought and didn't need to drink mine. I was dancing with the host when we happened to dance near Archie, I heard Archie say that he didn't want kids.

I left our host in the middle of the dance floor, picked up my drink—almost pure rye—and downed it. The next thing I remember is crawling on all fours, and trying to say the Lord's Prayer. Then, I was sitting on the throne with my head in the sink in front of me, both ends emptying. I was told later that if I had not done that, I might have died of alcohol poisoning. I didn't touch rye for a long time after that. Also never downed an alcoholic drink again. I found out that I had heard only part of a sentence that Archie had said. He was saying that he hadn't wanted children when we were first married. Not that he didn't want to have kids *ever*. I also learned not to listen to only part of a conversation and react, or even listen in on someone's conversation. At least to reserve what I think is being said until I know the whole story. I could have died for jumping to a conclusion. Good lesson to learn even though it was hard to take.

Another lesson my Mom taught me was to like someone for myself, not because Dad didn't. He didn't like a certain family and I was told not to have anything to do with them. When Dad wasn't around, I would hang around with one of the boys in that family until Dad caught me one day and that was the end of it for a while.

I didn't find out that Dad was prejudiced and thought that French people were the only "good" people. One evening when we were celebrating my sister's engagement to a Frenchman, Dad said something—he was drunk—about at least *someone* in this family is marrying French. I don't know what else he said because I wasn't in the room. Archie came in and said he wanted to go home, that he wasn't wanted here. I got into the next room just in time to hear my father's nephew's wife, who was pure Irish, really telling my father off. My father had forgotten that she also was not French. I didn't understand, at the time, because Dad and Archie were best friends and drinking buddies. They continued to be best friends and drinking buddies after that night. Dad always took Archie's side if anyone would say or do anything against him. He kicked my brother Oscar, who was still living at home with his family, out when he said something against him. I knew then not to say anything against Archie in front of Dad because he probably would take his side against me.

For the first few months of our marriage, I wondered why I wasn't getting pregnant. I thought that if I had sex, I would get pregnant. I was sure there was something wrong. We both went to a doctor and we were told that Archie could not father children. Shortly after that I became pregnant. It became a bone of contention between us. I was accused of being unfaithful and he even accused the poor ten-year-old boy who used to deliver our newspaper. The accusations did not stop until our daughter, Annette was born. I had not even thought of being unfaithful and go outside my marriage at that time. After all, we had just gotten married.

When my brother-in-law wanted to bet with me that I was having a boy, I refused to bet with him because I didn't think it was fair. I said I knew I was having a girl when I was pregnant for my first. It wasn't because the doctors told me or I had had an ultra sound. I didn't have any ultra sound with my first pregnancy. It was considered dangerous for the baby at that time. I just knew. I KNEW I was having a girl.

When Archie came in to see us in the hospital the first time there was a smile on his face that I had never seen on him before or after. A smile that said to me that he was so well pleased and happy. She was 8 lbs. 15 oz. The biggest baby in the hospital that year, 1967. It was Centennial year and we called her our Centennial baby. My stay in the hospital was a whole week. I couldn't sit down without a special pillow with a hole in it. I needed blood transfusions. Remember I was a bleeder.

The doctor told Archie that I wasn't to get pregnant within the next year because it was dangerous for me. Don't tell an alcoholic that he cannot do anything. I became pregnant but lost the baby on October 26, 1967 on the way to the city Health Centre clinic for Annette's checkup. This was for Annette's needle and to see how she was doing at three months. I stayed home from work for the first six months after Annette was born, which was the way it was then. The only thing was, there was no pay. I returned to work but after a day and a half I couldn't do it. I was away from my baby and I was a mess. I was told to go home and be with her. I quit my job and stayed home. Unemployment insurance helped so I stayed on it until it ran out.

We had a small dog and were living in an upper duplex when Annette was born. The woman who lived downstairs didn't like dogs and she put in a complaint to the landlord that our dog had peed on the veranda and it had come through onto her clean clothes hanging on her clothes line right under our veranda. Archie brought our dog to the dog pound. The next day I poured dirty water onto our veranda right over her clothes line. The landlord came storming into our apartment to tell us. By that time, I was looking for another place to move to. I told the landlord that we had gotten rid of our pet and that the woman had lied that the dog wasn't around to do what she said he did.

We moved to live with Archie's cousin and his wife. An apartment was to be made in the basement for us and while it was being done, we stayed in the one bedroom in the house with our furniture being stored in the basement. The apartment was never built. We were living here when I became pregnant and lost the baby. After that I was sick for months and when I finally went to the doctor, he told me that I was pregnant again. As I had not missed any of my monthlies, I couldn't be pregnant but he insisted that I was four months pregnant. I called him every nasty name—to his face—that I couldn't be but it didn't change the fact. To this day, I don't believe that I was four months pregnant, maybe pregnant but not four months. At four months a woman can usually feel the baby and I didn't feel it. Six months later my second daughter was born.

Annette was still a baby and one night I needed to pick up some jewellery that I was selling by having home parties and then to pick up some flash bulbs for my camera at the new K-Mart on the way home. I left Annette with Archie expecting to be home on time for the 10:00 p.m. feeding. My purse strap was broken and I carried my purse in my hands. That meant I only had one hand to shop with. K-Mart didn't have carts yet so I had to hold everything in the hand I was shopping with or put it in my purse and take it out at the cash. I had done that many times before. I did that at the cash but forgot the small package of flash bulbs for my camera at a cost of $1.23. As soon as I stepped out of the store, I got picked up. The security woman treated me roughly or as I used to say, like a criminal. Now, I understand because she thought I was. I was brought to a room and the police were called. I asked if I could call my husband and told them that I had a small baby at home that needed to be fed. They allowed me a phone call but I wasn't allowed to say anything except that I would be late and could he feed the baby and told him how to do it. He wasn't to know that I had been arrested. I was then taken to the police station and fingerprinted. They brought me back to my car at K-Mart and I went home.

I told Archie and his cousin what had happened. His cousin called his brother-in-law, who was a policeman and he came over. He got me a court date and I had to go to that.

When I went to court, I was given a court-appointed lawyer. I told him everything and when I was put on the stand, I answered the questions as was asked. Having sworn an oath on the Bible to tell the truth, the whole truth and nothing but the truth, I did. When I was asked if I had stolen anything before, I had to say, "Yes." I could see my lawyer slouch down in his seat. As the prosecutor asked more questions my lawyer slouched down farther and farther until I could only see his eyes above the table in front of him. I knew he didn't like me saying what I did, but I had to tell the truth. After the prosecutor was finished asking questions I turned to the judge and asked,

"Your Honour, can I ask a question?"

He said, "Yes, you can."

So, I did. I asked, "Where is the shopping centre in Osgoode?"

He asked, "Why?"

I told him that the woman security guard had accused me in being well known to steal from the shopping centre in Osgoode. There was no such thing as a shopping centre in Osgoode. He also asked me if I had stolen the flash bulbs and I told him that no but I had forgotten them in my purse, that I had used my purse as a hold-all before and hadn't forgotten anything. I had my husband's pay cheque and mine in my purse plus money from the sale of my jewellery. I also had the new jewellery that I had just picked up from the office.

At the end of everything the judge dismissed the charge of shoplifting and threw it out of court. Also, I learned later that the security guard had been fired. There is no record of it today.

Chapter 8

CRIPPLED

Archie had a car accident and our car was demolished. He had no way to go to work so we moved to the farm to my mom's and dad's. He and my brother Oscar found a job at a Hydro company in a town about an hour and one half from home and so he moved there leaving me at the farm because I was pregnant and there were no hospitals within an hour's drive from where he was. His alcoholism escalated as he was alone in the bush with other guys and didn't have much to do—I was told—so they drank and played cards.

Being pregnant for Caroline, Archie working away from home, and Mom in the hospital, I was living back at home with Annette. One day I was sweeping the floor in the kitchen when Dad came in from the barn and told me to put the broom down, that I wasn't to be doing that. He wouldn't let me sweep the floor because I was pregnant. I found out that he didn't believe a pregnant woman was to do any housework. I later asked Mom how she did the housework with Dad around and she told me that was why she had it done before he came home from work. If he was home and it needed to be done, she would have us do the work. Now I understood. I would do it when Dad wasn't around after that. Also, I wasn't allowed to ride my bike to go to the village, two miles away. I would put Annette in the basket and bike to the store. After he caught me one day, I had to push the carriage with her in it all the way to the village. On a dirt road, it was a lot harder and seemed a lot longer that if I was on the bike.

According to the doctor's calculations, I was almost a month overdue when the time approached and went to have the baby. The next appointment he told me to drink a small bottle of castor oil to bring the baby on. I drank it, but the only thing it did was have me sit on the toilet for the night. Two weeks later, he told me to do it again. This time Mom wouldn't let me. She gave me two tablespoons only. That was enough to repeat the last time. Nothing. Then, when the baby was ready, I woke up with labour pains. They were one minute apart. I told my mom, she called for the ambulance, she made me breakfast, and I ate it, while we waited for the ambulance.

When the ambulance came into the yard my dad came hopping from the barnyard and said, "Why didn't you tell me? I could have driven her to the hospital." At that moment, I could just see Dad driving faster than it was safe to do so and panicking. I answered him. "I want to get there safe, not in an accident."

The driver asked if anyone is going with me and I said no. My dad said, "Yes, her mother is going with her." Mom was not dressed to go anywhere and she didn't have her purse but Dad made her come with us. She had no way home or any money with her at the hospital. We were only halfway to the hospital when the baby was born. One and a half hours only in labour from the first pain to the last. Going through the emergency at the hospital I could see everyone looking at us. The baby was on the outside of the blanket on top of me. Why was she not covered? I didn't get to see her again for a few days because she, being born in the ambulance, the nurses were making sure she was alright before they brought her to me.

Our second daughter, Caroline, was born, weighting 8 lbs 1 oz. It was known by everyone at Archie's work that he was waiting for his second child to be born. There was only one telephone in the village and the operator told someone when my mother called to tell Archie that I had the baby. By the time the news got to Archie everyone else knew it. They bought him drinks and he handed out cigars until he finally started for home in the evening. He got to the hospital at 7:30 in the morning to see me. He was disappointed that she wasn't a boy. He had wanted a boy so bad that he didn't have much to do with her for quite a while. He never went back to work there.

By the time he was finished with that company I noticed that he had become almost obsessed with drinking. We were still living at my mother's and I started to go to bingo in the village. Archie would drive me there, drop me off, and was to pick me up when the bingo was over. Many nights, he would be late or not pick me up at all. I would have to walk the two miles home in the dark. Sometime during the night he would show up drunk.

One night he didn't come home at all. My mom and I called everywhere, the hospitals, police, everywhere we could think of. When he finally came home later in the day, he told us that he was on the Quebec side and was arrested and put in jail. He had been driving drunk and was stopped. Not understanding French, he fought the police. We later had to go to court there. This was the beginning of a merry-go-round of drinking, disappearing, fights, and a lot of the word "divorce" being thrown around; all this went on for years. We moved often because of not being able to pay the rent, including moving back to the farm.

I became crippled from Rheumatoid Arthritis when the girls were about one year and six months old. Archie would carry me wherever I had to go. I felt useless having to be carried and not being able to walk on my two feet. Also not being able to look after my own girls didn't help my self-esteem and self-worth either. When I had to go to the hospital outpatient appointments, he would carry me in and put me in a wheelchair, then put the girls on my knees because I couldn't run after them if they got away from me. He would go to work and come back at noon to pick me up and drive me to his parents' home, who had moved into the city by then. I felt that everyone was looking at me being carried and pitying me.

Archie paid a girl to come to look after the girls and me and to do housework but she didn't look after the girls or do housework. That weekend, it took Archie a day and half to clean the house, the girl's room—they had soiled their bed and rubbed it all around their cribs—and by Sunday afternoon I told him to take a break. He took the girls, went to visit Mom and Dad, and when he came back, he brought my brother William back with him. William told me that he would take over and he would look after the girls and me.

The next morning, I woke up hearing arguing in the kitchen. It seems that no one had told the previous helper that she was fired. She was insisting on coming into the bedroom to find out what was going on, but my brother wouldn't let her. He told her that I wasn't awake yet and he wasn't going to wake me up. This girl was his girlfriend and they broke up that day.

That day I had fried chicken for lunch, the girls were fed and the house was clean when Archie got home from work. We were well looked after. He stayed a few weeks and I never had to worry about the housework or the girls.

By the winter, I was a little better and at least was able to drag myself around. It was a slow process dragging my feet to be able to walk and pulling the sleigh with the girls on it to go to the store. I was so drugged up with the medication that the doctor gave me for the pain that I really didn't know what I was doing most of the time. The more exercise I did the better I got. A physiotherapist came to the house and gave me certain exercises to do. She also said that I would stay paralyzed for life if I followed the doctor's instructions of no stairs, no sweeping and to do nothing. She said I could do it but only a little at a time and slowly. I also couldn't pick up the baby to feed her the bottle. I didn't have feelings in my hands and arms to know if I was pushing the bottle too hard in her mouth. I positioned her in her car bed and put the bottle in her mouth. After about a year going to the arthritis doctor, I got better and the doctor wasn't sure that I even had rheumatoid arthritis. I continued to do the exercises the physiotherapist had me do and today there is no after effect of the disease at all.

We had to move out of this house. The landlord wanted to sell the house to us but we didn't have the money for the down payment. We moved back to Mom's and Dad's and lived in a tent in the yard since it was summer but we needed someplace for the winter, so Mom called the radio station to have them announce that we needed a place to rent.

Archie was good to me in those days. He only drank on Friday nights and weekends then. But the alcoholism progressed to the point that we were not getting along very well and fighting most of the time. The word divorce was thrown around like a football almost every time we fought to the point that our oldest daughter asked me one day, she was in her early twenties by then, *when are we going to divorce*? My answer to her was, "I didn't leave him during the bad days. I'm not leaving him in the good days. I want to enjoy the good days."

We got a call for a place for free rent for three months if we cleaned it up. Sounds good but it took a lot of elbow power, cleaning stuff and energy to do so. The old farmhouse had no heat, no insulation, not much of anything except baked-on dirt upon dirt. We got the walls in smallest room cleaned but couldn't get the ceiling cleaned. We made the smallest room a kitchen using the closet to put our canned goods in. There were no shelves so we put the canned goods on the floor. The cellar was infested with large rats so most of our food was in cans. Mom said that rats couldn't get through the cans. She was wrong. They did. One night, I was woken up by the sound of the double barrelled shotgun being fired from our bed. We slept downstairs to keep the wood stove going to keep it warm. Archie had woken up when a rat had run across our bed so he was shooting at them.

Archie would go to work and I'd be there with our two young girls with no way of contacting anyone if something were to happen. It did. One day I heard a noise in the next room and went out to see. It was a pig and I chased it out but as I did, I fell through the floor. The rotted floor boards gave way, and I got stuck there, caught up to my waist, for the rest of the day. That part of the house didn't have a basement, it was just the ground under it. Thank God for that or I could have gotten hurt much worse. Our girls at that time were only about two and three years old, not old enough to understand, so when Archie did get home from work that night, they were crying and I imagine, hungry. I had tried to get out of the hole but had scratched myself until I bled. That is how Archie found me.

There was a room upstairs that we kept the door closed because there was a raccoon in it. He would come in at night and we would hear him moving around in there. He would leave in the daytime and we tried to cover where he came in but every night, he removed it and came in anyway. We found another place to live and moved into the village again.

Money meant more to me than anything else. It had become my god. I was only going to pay for whatever I had to and really needed. I was very careful to count to the penny what was given to me. A few times, my husband would walk out on me from a grocery store because of me causing a disturbance. He was ashamed to be with me. Once, a cashier ripped me off of one penny and I demanded for her to give it to me. She denied it and an argument became loud. I wanted everyone to know that she was trying to rob me. Another time, a woman took a frozen turkey out of my basket and I wanted it back. I called for the manager and again loudly demanded that she was to return it. It had been the last turkey in the store. Still another time, I wanted hamburger meat and had my own idea of exactly what it was. Beef only. There were different kinds of hamburger meat, the butcher said. Some had soy in it and I didn't want anything but plain minced beef. They didn't have any. I would not pay for anything else. That time the police were called in, it got so bad. I had everyone that had already had meat, of any kind, in their baskets put it back on the shelves. I was telling them that it was not pure meat if it was meat at all. The manager called in the owner of the store and he called the police. Archie, of course was waiting in the car, and expected to see me being dragged off by police. I wasn't.

Now pennies don't exist. I pay mainly by credit card now. Back then I wouldn't have a credit card because I wasn't willing to throw money away by paying interest. Today I still don't pay interest. I pay the total when the bill comes in and there is no interest unless I carry a balance. Also, I no longer have the fear of being without and the anger that came with it. Those days are long in the past and hopefully never come back. I was such an unhappy, angry person then. People would say to me, "Do you ever smile?" and I would reply, "There's nothing to smile about." I thought my life was so bad. Today, I am mostly a happy, peaceful, and joyful person. After I started to recover in the Program I was asked, "How come you are always smiling?" What a turnaround! Today I have no reason to be sad or not smiling.

With everything that was going on in my life I became a 'worry wart'. I was using 'what if' so often that it got to the point that everything was so negative and I was afraid of doing anything. What if I did it wrong? What if something goes wrong? Why is he not home yet? Was he in an accident? What if they don't like me? It went on and on. I would worry about everything. I have wasted so much of my life by needless worry. It really got me nowhere and most of the 'what ifs' never happened. If they did, I couldn't have done anything about it in the first place. Now, if I find myself thinking 'what if', I know I am on the wrong track and need to turn my thinking to Jesus and whatever I was thinking about, hand it over to Him and let Him handle it. I could be doing something more constructive with my life.

I returned to the work force in 1971. This time I worked for DND (Department of National Defence) and worked in that department for twenty-three years. I started as a typist in a typing pool and from there was moved to the Orderly Room (OR). The other typists were getting the best jobs and another girl and I were getting the junk jobs to type. One Friday afternoon, my friend said we should do what the other girls are doing. We were older and wearing dresses down to our knees and seeing that the younger girls, who were wearing miniskirts got the good jobs. The style was hot pants suits in those days. Hot pants suits were a pair of short panties with a short skirt that barely covered your bottom. The bottom of the skirt ended at the very bottom of your butt. There was no bending over with hot pants.

She said that we should go out, shop and buy a few hot pants suits and wear one on Monday. I wasn't sure but since I said I would do it, I did go shopping and bought two suits and wore one on Monday. She had done the same. It didn't take long when I noticed we were getting some of the good jobs as well. Along with that came the attention, which I didn't like. When the other girls moved to other floors to work, I stayed in the Orderly Room.

One day, the captain standing behind me was dictating as I was typing. I was sitting on a low back swivel chair. He pressed himself up against the back of the chair and forward enough to be also against my back. I took it for a while until I was finished typing and then took action. I swivelled around really fast with my elbow out behind me and struck him just in the right place to do the most harm. He bent over and yelled. The master corporal, who I presumed, had been watching asked him what was wrong. I noticed his face and knew he had seen what had happened. The captain never tried again. The other girls used to ask me how come I never get bothered in that way and I said, "I don't know." I never told them of that time with the captain.

I applied for a competition that was in the same building but instead it turned out to be elsewhere. I won that competition and changed to work in the films department. I started here as a typist and entered another competition and became a film reviser. Here I had to run the films through a revising machine and find places where the sprockets (holes in the films that pass through the projector) were ripped, and cut off the parts that were damaged and splice it together again. To glue the film together I had to use a toxic product. Eventually, it was changed to film cement that wasn't toxic. Then someone higher up thought that we could be in the same section as the training publications since we had training films for the military. We were moved and joined the publication part of the department. We moved to the base to join them.

After a few years, I became a clerk in receipts, doing paperwork and computer work. Computers were new to us and when I was told that I would be using one, I was scared of it. I took night classes to learn a word-processing computer course. That was once per week for three months. When I was put on the computer at work, I was put with another supervisor to teach me what I needed to do. That was a six-month course. I was also sent to a two-day computer course to learn about how to use and navigate the computer screen and what I would need to know to do my job. At work during the lunch hour, I would play games to get over my fear of the computer. I was told that I couldn't damage it or break it.

Eventually, I bought a second-hand computer for my home to practice on and within a month I had done something to it that it was no longer useful. I bought a brand new one and within a few months, I had crashed the hard drive. It was impossible to repair. I couldn't tell you what I did with either one to damage them to become unusable. To this day I and the computer have a love/hate relationship. When it works well, all is well; but when it doesn't, things are not so well.

Here I had a chance to become an acting supervisor and a proof reader—comparing the printed pages to the original. I would mark and send back what needed to be reprinted. Each substitute job was for three or six months. I learned a lot in these different jobs. Like when you are a supervisor, you are responsible for who you supervise. When the girl didn't do the job, I gave her to do, I did it. Not my job, it was hers. I was to make sure she did it, not take over. Crap comes down the ladder, I was told. It did.

I was in trouble for doing someone else's job. My job was to see to it that *she* did it, not *me*. I remembered that when she substituted for the next three months and she became my supervisor for three months.

While I was working for the Department of National Defence I learned to Curl. I did enjoy curling but we did it only once a year. It was an all-day event— tournament among my co-workers. Sometimes I was on the winning team, sometimes not. We would have parties now and then for the afternoon but we all had to have all our work caught up before we could go. One afternoon, as I was leaving the base, I was stopped by police on a road check. The policeman asked if I had anything to drink. Without thinking I said, "Yes, water." The policeman thought I was being smart. This was the first time that I had been stopped in this type of check. I told him that I was only answering his question. Did I have anything to drink? I had been drinking water only at the party. He let me go.

After my mom was remarried and moved to a town nearby, she was playing darts in the Legion and so I joined that as well. I enjoyed it and the time with Mom on those nights.

I used to go to the bingo three times a week. It only cost me $3.50 for the night unless I wanted to play with more cards for the special games. I would play twenty-one cards for the regular games. I would only win enough to go another night and I continued that for three or four years. I went to different bingos in the area and sometimes in the city. I became addicted to trying to win big but as most gamblers, I never did. When I noticed that I had become addicted, I quit completely. I knew that I couldn't just slow down and go once in a while. It was quite a few years before I did go one night to a turkey bingo one Christmas to win a turkey for a family that couldn't afford a Christmas dinner. Our part was to supply the turkey for the dinner basket. That night, I won three turkeys. One for the basket, one for us, and I gave one to someone else. I have not gone to a bingo since.

I also had to be careful when I started taking my mom and step dad to the casino every week. At first, I didn't play and then they got me in their club which meant that I got a $15 voucher to play every week when I brought them so I played with that. There were times that I was tempted to use some of my own money but I knew that if I did it once it may get out of hand. I joined another club and I got a $20 voucher from them and was able to play with $35 that week and every week. If I won some money, I would keep it. I didn't gather points to make any money of my own (we would get points to convert to money if we spent enough). After Mom passed away, I went a few weeks but gambling alone was not fun any longer and I haven't been back to that either.

Chapter 9

SHOT

One of the jobs Archie had was a job cleaning portable toilets on construction sites. Sometimes I would go with him if he had to work in the evenings. When I was finished work, I would go wait for him at the office where all the trucks were returned after their day. I got to know the men who worked with him. A few nights that he worked and I was with him, we left the car at the office. We would do a few jobs and then when I got home, I had to deliver my Avon orders. I was an Avon representative. I only had the truck that Archie drove with the barrels on the back to deliver them. We called it the "Honey Wagon" which sounded better than what it was, and what it carried. It was a joke as well as I handed over the orders to my customers.

When the boss had a Christmas party at his home, we were invited. I was really nervous to have to go to a party with a lot of rich people. The first thing the boss's wife did was make me feel welcomed and confided in me that she was also uncomfortable around the "rich" people. Attending that party were the owners and their wives of a few of the major construction companies in the city and area. We were just sitting around and no one was doing much else but talking to each other. Some of the bosses were in the makeshift room in the garage, where card games were going on. I wanted to play cards so I asked my husband about it. He said, "You can't afford to play cards with them." He told me to go ahead and see. I did. As I walked into the room, I saw one man lay down a $100 bill and then another man lay down another $100 bill. There were stacks of bills on the centre of the table. I looked over at the other table where the kids were playing and there were only pennies on the table. That was more like me, playing cards for pennies. I think if there had been another adult at that table, I would have joined the kids, but there wasn't. I turned around and went back into the party.

We were asked to start dancing and hopefully, others would join in. They finally did. When the party was over most of the people went home. Only one other couple stayed to help clean up. We helped clean up and the boss's wife told me that we didn't have to. No one ever stays to help out. She would do it herself. We stayed until most of it was done. There was a lot of food leftover and she gave us some to take home for staying to help. After that party, Archie and I talked about it and figured out that the rich are no different from us. We had been better dressed than most of them at the party. The boss's father was bragging about buying the suit, which he was wearing, at the thrift shop.

On a Good Friday in April, Archie spent the day fighting fires and after he got home, two friends and Archie, decided to go pick up a case of beer. Somehow, they landed in the city and were in a car chase and when they were stopped, Archie was shot in the face.

I got the phone call late at night from the hospital to ask me what could have been on the dash of the car that could have gone up his nose when the car crashed. I called my mom, and she and my brother drove me to the hospital. My sister babysat the girls. The next day, I went to pick up the car at the police pound and there wasn't a scratch on it. There had not been a crash, as the hospital was told.

My father-in-law drove me and when we were in the garage getting the car he said to me, loud enough for the policeman to hear, "You will have to buy a gun to protect yourself." He went on and on, so to shut him up I said, "I have one in my purse," without thinking of what the policeman would do to me. My father-in-law left as I got in the car to drive out and the policeman wanted to see my gun. I showed him the starter pistol that I carried around with me. It looked like a real gun so the policeman told me not to ever pull it out if I was really in danger because the other person may have a real one and I could be the one shot. I quit carrying it after that. I gave it to someone who collected guns.

I later found out that Archie had been shot in the face. The bullet went in by the side of his nose, ricocheted off the spine and lodged just under his ear. The next day by the time I got to the hospital he was on his way to the operating room. I stayed with him the rest of the day. I went to see him every day. While I was in the room with him, I felt better but started worrying when I was away from him. Because the doctors could not get all the bullet fragments out, there were fragments of the bullet in his neck the rest of his life. The powder burns on the side of his nose were visible for years after. The hole wasn't visible but the powder burns were. He wasn't to jar his neck so the fragments would move. They told me that it could kill him. I was so fearful that someone would make him move his neck suddenly and jar the fragments. I lived with that fear for a few years.

He left the hospital with a full body cast from his waist to the top of his head. There was a hole over his stomach, so he could breathe and part of the front of his head and his face. His arms were out from his side past the holes on the side. He had that cast on for about six months. When they took it off, they weighted him with it on and then off. With it on he was 185 lbs. but only 115 lbs. with it off. The doctor told me to watch and hang on to him when we got outside because there was a small breeze and he might blow over. He had been carrying 70 lbs. of cast for so long that he had to learn to stay upright again without it. Sure enough, when we got outside, I had to hold him up. I hardly felt the breeze but it was like a strong wind to him.

The girls were in school and they had a class called 'show and tell'. They would have to bring something to school to show and tell all about it. One of the girls decided that they would have their dad as show and tell. She told the class about him getting shot in the face and that he still had part of the bullet in his head. One of the students yelled 'If he had been shot, he would be dead'. Her answer was, 'Can't you see he is not dead? He didn't die'. He became a hero to those little kids in her class. I was surprised that he would allow himself to be used as a 'show and tell' object, but that is what he was like. Doing whatever he could for his girls even if it was an embarrassment.

While he was in the cast and for a while after it came off, he couldn't go to work. During the summer, he had the girls to look after so he had something to do. He would take them to the ball diamond at the Community Centre and play ball with them and their friends. It kept him busy but at other times he drank. His boss would come stay with him for an afternoon quite often. He also took him back when he was ready to go back to work. The boss was a good friend to him until the business was sold. The deal included that Archie would keep his job and go with the new boss but it wasn't the same. Finally, Archie was let go or he quit, I don't remember now.

Having moved a few times, we bought a house next door to where we were living. Here, for the first time, the girls each had their own separate bedrooms and we could do what we wanted in the house, like paint, build or take out walls—which Archie did to make the living room a little larger. I paid the down payment with the money I made at my second job—a beauty counsellor. Archie paid the mortgage. I paid all the other bills. It worked out until he got bad enough in his disease of alcoholism that we didn't have the money some months to pay the mortgage.

It got that I was coughing and choking so much while at work that the other girl who worked at the next desk asked to be moved. She was pregnant and it was affecting her. She said it made her stomach sick and she couldn't concentrate. I had been going to all the doctors I was sent to but they couldn't find what was wrong. Work sent me to Health and Welfare Department and I went through all their doctors, psychotherapist, psychoanalyst, psychiatrist, etc. But nothing. A few years later I was sent again and went through it all again.

At work, we were changing the system to hold only one of each publication with a scanned book to reprint it when needed. Scanners were not heard of in homes yet, only in the industry. When they decided to do it at night as well, they asked for volunteers to work on the new scanner. I volunteered and for the last few months I worked night shift scanning with only one other person in the building.

The doctor wanted me to quit my job because of my health, but I thought that if I worked away from people who wore perfume, my coughing would become better, but it didn't. I found out that it was also the ink that I was allergic to. I had to quit. The doctor wrote me a letter for work. That was in 1994. I was put on disability insurance for twenty-four months. That was the long-term insurance I had. Then it stopped. I tried to get on again but couldn't. I became determined to do without it and became very careful with my money and what we had. I learned to make do and if I wanted more, to find a way to make the money for it.

About three or four years previously all the girls where I was working were knitting something so I decided to knit too. In the fall, I started knitting pullover sweaters for my mom, Archie, and our two girls for Christmas presents. We had started going back to church every Sunday and going to a breakfast meeting right after. By the time we got home it was afternoon. I would then knit the sweaters I was making and continued to knit until I had too many done with nowhere to put them. It was suggested to me to go to craft fairs with them and sell them. I did.

At first it was only sweaters but soon I started doing other crafts, mostly using recycled materials. Buttons became earrings, and from there it branched out into a lot of other crafts and things including homemade fudge, zucchini bread and jams. After I retired, medically, I took on more and more craft fairs and one table at the farmers market every Saturday. It became a business and started making the crafts in bulk. When I quit at the market, I found that I wasn't as interested in doing the crafts any longer. It was because I had turned it into a business. I had had a dream of starting a craft store but never got there nor ever made any money at it. My mother was good at doing so many things. Some of the things she did was crochet, sew and draw pictures. I tried and tried to do as good as she had in drawing pictures but never could achieve it like she did. I get the love of doing crafts from her and my daughters also got it.

My youngest daughter, Caroline, painted pictures and became good at it. For her birthday and Christmas, I always knew what she wanted. Oils, canvas and any supplies for her paintings. We encouraged her as much as we could. She was good and had a commission to paint a wooden plaque for a business that was newly opened in the village. She painted in oils and now draws portraits of people and animals. She makes a little bit of money doing it the same as Mom made with her crocheted items.

My focus was so much on her achievements that I failed to see that my older daughter, Annette could also draw. I found some of her drawings after she passed away. She was also good at it.

When I was in the Catholic Church, I heard of some of the women going on a trip to Ste Anne de Beaupre for the weekend. I had read about Ste Anne in a book and decided that I would go. It was a pilgrimage, which I wasn't sure what that was at the time, but I did enjoy it. I was with a friend's mother and we stayed in the same room for the weekend. This experience was completely new to me. I depended on her to let me know what to do and where to go. She had been there a few times. We split up during the day but she told me where to be at a certain time and what I needed to go see.

On the way to Ste Anne's, we stopped at Cap de la Madeline. There was a lot to see there and we had to attend mass in a huge cathedral. There was one church with a pure gold (I was told) altar, but you couldn't get near it because there was a large chain to stop visitors from doing so. The cathedral was beautiful with high ceilings, colourful statues, and fancy carvings on the walls. The Cathedral at Ste Anne's was just as beautiful. The thing that I noticed even more, was how many stores there were—booths with religious things to sell. Being my first time, I came home with a bagful of trinkets, something for everyone I wanted to give something to.

I took a few trips after that year but didn't buy as much as I did the first trip. I spent more time in places I didn't have time to the first year because I was afraid to miss something. Now I knew what to expect. One of the events no one should miss is the candlelight vigil. It is beautiful as everyone, holding a lit candle, makes their way in a line up throughout the grounds of the cathedral. One year, I was sick and stayed in my room and missed it. The two women that I was rooming with wanted to stay with me but I told them they had to go. It was something they couldn't miss. They were glad they went. It turned out that something I ate made me sick and I was OK the next day.

On one of the trips Archie and I took, I wanted to show him what it was like there so we detoured and went. The whole town seemed different. There were a lot fewer booths and stores. Even the church inside seemed to be different. We agreed that the place was set up when a pilgrimage was expected to maximize sales and to accommodate a lot of people at one time.

Because I was very insecure—I learned that much later in life—I became very, very jealous. Archie couldn't look towards another woman that I didn't react. A lot of the times when I did, it wasn't pretty. I would accuse him of something or attack the other person verbally for trying to get my husband and told her to get her hands off, in no uncertain terms. A lot of the times, the other woman had no idea what I was talking about. He would turn and look towards the door and I would react thinking he was going to go out again to drink or be with someone else. I would start yelling at him about wanting to get away from me. Now, looking back, I would have wanted to get away from me too. I was that bad. It got so bad and I was so unhappy that Archie didn't want to even know me or be with me in public. He wasn't doing anything wrong and down deep I knew it but I didn't trust other women around him. I figured I had nothing good to hold him. I wasn't a good enough wife, good looking enough, good housekeeper, good enough mother, or good enough at anything. The more I tried the more I would think I was not good enough. By the time I hit my bottom and had nowhere to go or to get help, I was really a basket case.

Chapter 10

Real Love

In November 1978, after a really big fight and still going to work that day, I made some phone calls and was led to call someone from a 12-step program for families of alcoholics. I started that Sunday night. I learned to focus on myself instead of others and look at my faults, not theirs, also to live one day at a time which took a lot of worry off my mind. I was burdened and unhappy with the past but I didn't have to fear tomorrow and to live for today only.

Matthew 6:34 Therefore do not worry about tomorrow, for tomorrow will worry about itself. Each day has enough trouble of its own.

It is truly freeing. I found I have a lot of faults and it was and still is a lot of work to change. I learned the 3 C's. 'I didn't Cause it, I can't control it, and I can't cure it.' I am powerless, so let go and let God do it. I choose Jesus as my higher power. This 12-step program is non-religious but is a spiritual program. I started going back to church and eventually reading the Bible, which led me to want more and more. It also enforced the 12-step program for me. Both programs have been taken from the Bible.

During the drinking years, I would sit by the window and watch cars go by, waiting to see our car coming up the street. To pass the time I would count cars and think when the tenth (or whatever number I thought of that night) car comes by it would be his car. Then when it didn't, I would start all over again. At the same time, I would think of what I would do to him when he got home, what could happen to him to make him late getting home—he hadn't been home from work yet —hoping that he hadn't been in an accident and the same time thinking, "I'm going to kill him when he gets home." Some nights I even planned how I would do it without getting caught. When he finally did come in the door, drunk out of his mind, the first thing out of my mouth would be, "Where the h.... have you been?" Now I think, that was the dumbest question to have asked. I knew where he had been. Drinking, and did it matter where? No! It didn't matter where. Of course, because of my attitude, tone of voice, and the question, an argument would start.

Yelling and accusations would fly. I would bring up the past and repeat everything he had done, even if it was years before. In most of our arguments, the word 'divorce' would be used and after a few minutes the end of the fight would end up with each of us going to bed. I would go to the bedroom and he on the couch. These fights would happen at least once or more per week until I had reached the lowest point in my life that I had to do something.

After starting in the Program, it took a while before I quit meeting him at the door when he got home. I went to bed as soon as I knew he was in the yard and pretended to be asleep when he came into the house. No more fights when he got home. At first, he thought he was in the wrong house—he told me that later when we discussed it—but eventually I was able to go to bed and sleep until some nights I didn't know when he got home. Arguments were not as often and I learned to "shut up". One of the slogans in the Program is "there is a time to be silent." That was too long for me to remember so I shortened it to "shut up". That I understood. Life became quieter at home.

"R*ecovery is a process. It takes time to regain, reclaim, and recoup all that was lost while we tried on our own to cope with active drinking" (*taken from *Courage to Change*). Today, I am still working on changing my thinking and do what I need to do to do it.

Archie started in the 12-step program for alcoholics in February of 1979. He didn't know I was going to a program because I changed from Sunday night to during the week in the day time. I would take time off work and go. I used up my annual leave by taking a quarter day of leave a week. After he was in the Program for about a year, I told him that I had been going since that Sunday night. Since he joined the Program, I didn't miss a week for years. At first, I would go to five meetings a week plus go with him to a meeting to support him but also to try to understand the alcoholic. It helped me a lot.

When we were first in the Programs, we would gather together with others in the Programs after the meetings for coffee and fellowship. Sometimes, these gatherings were better than the actual meetings we had just come out of. The second meetings, the gatherings, brought us together to talk and we would talk about anything that was bothering us. Not being in a formal meeting, we could just talk and help each other. When it was at our place, I would make the first pot of coffee and serve everyone. After that, I told them that if the pot was empty someone else was to make the coffee and everyone was to help themselves. Some nights, we would go through five or six pots of coffee depending on how many people there were. I could drink numerous cups of coffee and still sleep at night. Now, I can't drink coffee after 12:00 noon and still can't get to sleep but I think it has nothing to do with coffee.

During the drinking years I became very angry and I dealt with everything with anger. Whether I was disappointed, sad, or whatever, it all came out in anger. By the time I got to the recovery programs—I was in more than one—I didn't know how I felt because all I knew was anger. That anger took a very long time to get rid of. I had to do a lot of work on myself and eventually it is almost gone. I did learn that it was OK to be angry but it is what I do with it that is important.

One of the ways I dealt with my anger at first was to pull the weeds in my flower beds. I had the cleanest flower beds around. I would pull the weeds out thinking I was pulling his hair out, or whoever I was angry with. Each weed I pulled, I took pleasure in feeling that I was causing pain and eventually I felt better. It was quite a few years before I was able to not have to pull weeds (someone's hair) out to get rid of the anger. I also didn't have to verbalize my anger because my body language would let people know I was angry. I would say "I'm not angry" but my body language would say "I'm very angry." I had to learn not to stuff my anger but to deal with it and change it. With God everything is possible.

Everything that happened that went wrong I blamed on someone else or something else, NEVER on me. It was never my fault. When I started to work on myself, I found that at least fifty percent of the time, if not all of it, I was responsible for. I started to look at my part in the things that went wrong and noticed that I wasn't right all the time or as perfect as I thought. Things in life got better for me when I put the focus on me, not on others. There weren't as many arguments any longer, and I was able to get along with Archie, and my girls, especially Annette more and even people I worked with.

Since I was little, I was a controller. I would manipulate the circumstance or person to get what I wanted or the way I wanted it to turn out. Until I got into the Program, I didn't know I was doing it but learned that I had become a master controller. This was one of the last things I wanted to let go because I was afraid of losing control of everything. I thought I needed to do it so things would not go wrong, but they did anyway. I found that I was not always right. Sometimes, even today, I have to be careful not to try to manipulate. I have to let people live their own lives and 'Let Go and Let God'. When I do that, things do turn out the way they should and eventually I do feel better. At least I don't feel bad about making the wrong decision.

At camping one weekend, things were getting out of hand with the drinking and my father-in-law, they were camping with us that weekend, in frustration turned to me and said, "Can't you control him?" My response to that was "I'm trying." I really thought that it was my job to keep him under control. My next comment wasn't very nice though. "You couldn't control him before I married him and now you want me to control him?" and then I went into my tent so angry and frustrated that all I could do was cry. Now I knew for sure that I wasn't good enough if I couldn't control his drinking and actions. Little did I know that it was all a lie and I stayed sick for a few more years until I was in the Program and I learned otherwise.

My attitude was so negative. Besides blaming things on everyone else or everything else, I would complain about it all. Instead of focusing on all the good things, I would focus and comment on the one or two times it was bad. For instance, the night Archie didn't come home instead of all the other times coming home safe. The girls never washed the dishes the way I wanted them to, so instead of being thankful that they *did* do them, I would yell and scream at them to do it right. Right meant *my* way. I am much better at it now but I still have to watch my tongue. I find that life is much happier when I think more positively and don't complain.

I was told that if I didn't have it, I couldn't give it away. Which means that if I didn't have recovery, I couldn't help anyone else. It also meant that if I didn't like or love myself, I wouldn't be able to love anyone. I remember a time that someone made me look in the mirror and told me to look myself in the eyes. What I saw there was really scary. After that, I tried a few times but was afraid to look inside myself. It was a long time before I was able to face myself in the mirror. I was scary to myself. I could only imagine what I looked like to others. I was seeing what I was really like inside. What were they seeing? The inside or outside? The outside was bad enough but if they saw the inside as well, I felt doomed. I had to change it and with God's help, I did. What I couldn't change, God changed. Now I like myself and can face myself in the mirror. I am becoming more who God has made me to be. I am not where I want to be yet but I am better than I was.

I found that I was changing for the better and my life wasn't as bad as I used to think. It was worth living and worth trying new things and seeing the beauty in things. I remember the evening I was driving home from work and noticed the trees changing colours in the fall. They were so beautiful that it took my breath away and I stopped the car right there by the side of the road to look at them. In awe I thought, "Wow, they must have looked like that every year in the fall, but I never saw it before." I started noticing the hummingbirds and put up a hummingbird feeder and spent time watching them. I started enjoying the flowers Archie had planted around the yard and when we bought our second home, I also helped keep the flower beds clean of weeds and admired the beautiful flowers.

When I was in grade 4 at Christmas, I was put in a play for the concert. Mom and all us kids walked through deep snow down our long lane way and the long trek to the school because I was in the play, but when I got up on stage that night I couldn't speak. Someone else had to say my part. In the 12-step Programs one of the things to do is to speak about ourselves for about forty minutes and tell what it was like, what happened, and what it is like now. My first time wasn't very long, but the more I did it the easier it got. I have spoken to my own group, other groups and at conferences where both groups meet. I found it hard to speak with alcoholics in the room, at first; but after a few times it got better. I was also able to share in a group anniversary with Archie at the meeting. We would each have to speak about twenty minutes. This helped me to be able to say anything in front of him and I hope helped him also. We didn't have secrets from each other. I used to say, "My life is an open book." Secrets make you sick. I find if I talk about something it loosens its grip on me.

When I got married, I really didn't know what love was or what it was all about. Only after Archie and I were in recovery I slowly learned love. Real love. The love that means a husband is not a possession but an equal. The love that you want the best for him, thinking of his needs instead of your own without leaving yourself out. Love that says "I love you" for how you really feel about him, NOT what you can get out from him or what he can do for you. Wanting to be with him, but letting him be himself, whether you like it or not. Letting him have an opinion not trying to change him but accept him for the way he is, not the way you want him to be. For the longest time I treated him as a possession the way I thought he should be. When I let him be himself, I found I really liked and loved him. He in turn did for me what I wanted him to do without asking or forcing him to do. Eventually I realized he was my Soul Mate. That is why I "stuck it out" with him through the hard times in the drinking years.

In public school, I was obsessed about being the best and tried to get the highest marks in my grade. I was comparing my marks with a girl who seemed to always get better marks than I did. If I got an 'A', she got an 'A'. When I got a 'B' she would get an 'A'. I would get angry at myself because I felt I wasn't as good as she was. She never knew that I compared myself to her. It seemed the harder I tried to beat her the more I failed to do so. Once in a while, I would get a slightly higher mark than she did and I remember that I thought myself better than her. I had to get a perfect mark because I wanted to be perfect. I was always judging myself and evaluating my worth by being the best in what I did. If I didn't do better than anyone else than I felt less than.

Perfection plagued me until I found out that I did not need to be perfect. Everything I did had to be perfect and I judged how other people did things and thought they were not doing it right. It had to be perfect. Now I know that I also thought of perfection as doing it my way. You know. My way was the right way. Later I learned that it wasn't, and some people can do it better than I can. Also, today I know that I know that God does a much better job of running my life than I could ever do. When

I ran my own life, look where it got me. In a lot of arguments, problems, and trouble, that I caused by thinking I knew better.

As I began to learn that I was as good as anyone else I also learned that no one else was better than, or lesser, than I. Someone once told me that I was perfectly made by God because He didn't make junk. I am NOT junk. God made each of us different but as good as the next person. He did not make us perfect. Only one was and is perfect and that is Jesus. That made quite a difference in me looking at myself. Comparing myself to others is not a good thing. We are all unique and have our own quirks and abilities. I also learned that God was not a punishing God as I had been told all my life. God is a God of Love and He would never punish me. Our DNA and fingerprints are all different and so are we. I am to be myself and not try to be anyone else.

Chapter 11

SALMON

A bowling alley was built in the village and a league started up. As a teenager I joined a bowling league when Mom and Dad joined. I was in that league until I moved to the city for work and then made a home when we were married. I did stay on as a spare and spared when I was at the farm. When we moved to the village the bowling alley had shut down and the league had moved to another bowling alley in another town. By this time, I was in the Program but I joined again because I enjoyed bowling. Archie and the girls would continue going to their meeting. Eventually the league asked me to go on the executive and asked me to be the secretary statistician. I was really scared that I couldn't do it but not being able to say no I took the position.

One night before bowling, I cooked a whole salmon in the oven. By the time it was time to eat before Archie and the girls were to leave to go to their meeting the salmon wasn't cooked right throughout. I cut off enough for us to have for supper and put the rest back in the oven to finish cooking. Since I didn't have much time before I had to leave to be picked up by the bus taking me to the bowling alley, I turned up the temperature in the oven.

At the edge of the village on the way home from bowling that night,, we smelled burned fish.. Getting closer to our place, the smell got stronger in the bus. We lived in the middle of the village. I realized then what it was. I had forgotten to shut off the oven and the salmon burned. Archie and the girls came home to a house full of smoke and opened up all the windows and doors to try to get the smell out and the whole village smelled it. Everyone knew that I had forgotten to turn off the oven. After that, when I got on the bus to go to bowl, they would ask me if I shut off the stove. It was quite a joke for *them* but I didn't think it was a joke. We could have lost everything. God had protected our home from catching fire. I made sure from then on to shut everything off before leaving the house. I would double check many times. It was years before I would buy and cook another salmon to eat.

At that time, I also volunteered my every noon hour and my breaks at work to run our canteen. On weekends, besides going to meetings, we would volunteer at our church, if they needed anyone to serve at a meal or do any physical work when we remodelled the hall. My every moment was being filled in by doing things for others, to which I couldn't say no.

Not being able to say no, I had taken on too much and was burning out. Also, I didn't know how to balance what to do and what not to do so I decided to say "no" to everything. I stopped doing the secretary statistician job but continued to bowl, stopped volunteering at work and the church and anything else that I had said yes to. I found myself still wanting to say 'yes' to some of the things I was asked to do but figured if I said 'yes' once I would go back to saying it for everything again and my health couldn't handle it. I just didn't know how to balance it all.

I didn't want to have another nervous breakdown. I had had the worse one before I joined the Program and I sure didn't want another one. That one was really bad. I didn't go to work and my supervisor called to tell me that my pay cheque was in, and wanted to know what to do with it. I told him that I didn't care what he did with it. He knew that money was everything for me at that time. He told me to get myself out of bed and get to the doctor. I did and asked for nerve pills. I had been on them many times before. As the doctor handed me the prescription he said, "You know, you have to relax for these to work." As sick as I was, I thought, "If I could relax, I wouldn't need these." They have been the last nerve pills I have ever and will ever take.

At one time I noticed that some of my birth control pills were missing. I knew my girls were too young to take them but couldn't figure out what was happening to them. I kept them close to me and in my purse. When at home or elsewhere I never let my purse out of my sight. After Archie sobered up in the Program, he told me that he was taking them because he thought that they would do something to give him a high but they hadn't.

Dad got sick but was still working at the co-op in the village. When he was told he had to quit work and didn't, the doctor took the matter in his own hands to fix that. He went to Dad's boss and told him that he would have to let Dad go because of his health. So, Dad was retired until he got a part time job as a commissionaire. That only lasted a few years and he got worse. Since he could no longer work, Mom found a job, babysitting and taking care of a house. There was no phone in that house and since there was no such thing as cell phones there was no contact with Mom while she was at work.

I got a call at work one day from Dad's doctor. They had been trying to get hold of him to have him come in to the hospital but there was no answer. They had tried numerous times during that day. Knowing that no one, unless we went to Mom's job location, could let her know that Dad needed to get to the hospital it was left to me. I was told, by the doctor to get Dad to the hospital as fast as I could. I called Dad to tell him to be ready but he didn't answer the phone. I left the city, drove to the farm and when I walked in the door, Dad was sitting on his chair in the kitchen not dressed to go anywhere. I was not happy and I told him so. I told him that I had to take time off from my work, drive all the way here and he wasn't ready to go? And another thing, why hadn't he answered the phone? He said that he knew it was the doctor and the doctor wanted him to go to the hospital. He didn't want to go to the hospital. I told him that I had also tried to call him but he hadn't answered my call either. There was no call display back then either.

With authority, as if I was speaking to a child, I said, "Go get dressed, I am driving you to the hospital." He went and got dressed. Knowing that Dad didn't like to be in a fast-driving car, I drove much slower than the speed limit. He grabbed the door handle and held onto it until we got to the hospital. He later told Mom that I had flown the car to the hospital. He reverted back to only speaking and understanding French. When he asked for his four boys, he had written off his middle son a long time ago, Mom and I had to translate for them. At that time, I still knew enough of French to do that. In September 1978, the day before he died, he said that he was going home the next day. We wondered for a long time after, why would he say that. Now I know he didn't mean the farm, he meant heaven. Mom agreed.

At the funeral parlour, I really felt alone. Archie was drinking and wasn't in the funeral parlour most of the time. Once when it came time to go to get something to eat, I went along with someone else. I realized much later, after I got in the Program, that it was his way of mourning his drinking buddy. He was actually missing him more than I was. We had talked about it after we were both in the Programs.

When Annette was nearly fifteen years old, we had no choice but to tell her to live somewhere else because of her drinking and her attitude and actions. I had to think of my husband, who was just getting sober, and our youngest daughter, Caroline, who I was trying to keep on the right track. I moved her to my mother's and she lived there until my baby sister, Rebecca came to visit from British Columbia. Annette went to live with her and decided to continue her schooling there. I was happy about that. But her drinking got worse and by the time she graduated, my sister Rebecca couldn't handle her any longer. Annette moved out and started living with someone who was against drugs, thank God, but he was also an alcoholic. I never met him but was told that he was older than us.

The first trip we ever took was going to British Columbia for Annette's graduation for June 4th, 1986. We planned to bring her back home with us so Archie built a 4' X 4'

X 4' wooden box and tied it to the roof of my car. It was a Chevette. The box was almost as big as the car. The girls at work laughed at it when they saw it, just before I left work to go on holiday. We were so nervous. Actually, I was scared stiff. Going so far away from home was really scary. We left home four days before, what we thought was a graduation ceremony, for a 2000-mile drive. With our daughter, Caroline, Archie and I, we took turns driving, stopping only for pit stops and to eat. We drove all night. We did make it but not without a lot of trouble. The first night we stayed at my brother's place which was almost a day from home, at that time. We then crossed onto the Sault Ste Marie bridge to the United States. We wanted to go that way because it looked like it would be the fastest way. Unfortunately, as we were crossing the bridge the vehicle in front of us threw a stone and it blew a hole in our radiator. Shortly after that we ran out of water and we saw the hole.

Archie used the pepper, that we had for our sandwiches, to block the hole. I was angry with him for using all the pepper, because I had no pepper for my tomato sandwiches that we made. The pepper held for about a day and then we had to find water fast. We stopped and got some from a ditch. Finally, we had to stop where there was no water and the hood was really steaming. A vehicle, coming towards us, stopped and asked if he could help. He got us water to get us to the next town and told us to go to a mechanic there and he could help us. It was lunchtime when we got to the garage and had to wait. The man repaired the radiator as well as he could and hoped that it would get us to where we were going. He called ahead to a friend of his and made arrangements for us to get a new radiator installed. His friend had moved into the town where we were going. I was worried because we had brought only a certain amount of money for our trip. I had not anticipated any problems.

We made it to a border to cross back into Canada but being night time it was closed. Since I thought we wouldn't make it on time, I took over driving, while Archie and Caroline slept, and drove throughout the night. Early in the morning we got to the next border and crossed. By then I was so tired that I didn't even know where I was and asked the border guard, "Is this the way to Canada?" I pulled over and had a sleep. When Archie woke up, he took over driving. We stopped for breakfast and had the largest meal that I have ever eaten, then and since. We ended up eating two breakfasts each, not knowing that we were ordering two meals. The way it was written on the menu, it looked like we were ordering sides to a meal but it was a complete meal also. We ate it all! That day we drove and had to stop a few times to change clothes. It was hot in one place, then cold, and then so hot again. This was June.

We made it to my sister's place after dark. The next night was the commencement to the graduation ceremony.

We didn't find out until that night that Annette hadn't graduated yet. She still had to do her exams and if we took her home when we left, she wouldn't graduate. We had to leave her behind. We had the new radiator installed and the price was less than we expected so we had enough money to make it home.

On our way home we stopped to see sights and took our time driving home. This time we travelled in Canada. We had a tent with us and stopped for the night. One place we stopped and camped in a campground where the ground was all clay. We didn't notice that, nor did we notice that where we put the tent it was indented ground. That night we had a rain storm. I have not heard thunder like I heard that night ever since. It came from two directions at the same time and seemed to meet in the middle and really was loud—remember I was terrified of thunder and lightning. By morning, my purse and air mattresses were floating. Everything was wet. Not having the time to dry it all, it wasn't fit to put up the next night to sleep in, so we drove throughout the night.

We stopped to visit a few museums and we spent a whole day in a zoo. I had never been to a museum or a zoo. When we were back in Ontario, we stopped at one of the Great Lakes and spent the day searching for nice rocks by the water side. That box on the roof of the car may not have been used to bring Annette's things back from British Columbia but it was still at least half full by the time we got home. We had picked up a lot of large cones and rocks while in British Columbia and in Ontario, along with souvenirs.

After being in the Programs for a couple of years and getting to know more people Archie got another sponsor. I was between sponsors at that time. (A sponsor is a person to have a confidential relationship with to share our experiences, strength and hope. A sponsee learns from a sponsor as well as a sponsor can learn from the sponsee. Everyone in the Programs is encouraged to get a sponsor to help to grow to become a better person and to deal with what we need to deal with.) I had confided in my sponsor something that had nothing to do with Archie. She told him, and Archie, as he should have, went to his sponsor and told him what happened. His sponsor told mine to lay off his sponsee. She wouldn't talk to me for the longest time after that. It took me a long time to trust in someone enough to find another sponsor, but I did.

Archie's sponsor rented a piece of property by a river with a garage on it. With all his sponsees and their wives, we formed a "Club". We each had to pay a fee to become members of the Club. We cleared the lot to make a place to put tents, trailers and have a large camp fire. The men also built a wharf and painted it. They used any leftover paint any one had, whatever the colour and painted it. We had the most colourful wharf on the river. We turned the garage into a place to meet, to repair things, having bean suppers and just to get together to talk. We would meet around the campfire and the first subject of the meeting was "What are you grateful for?" then we would go around again with another subject. Most of those meetings lasted for at least two to three hours. If it went on too long some people went home but most of us stayed. Besides the members of the Club, other Program people would come for the meeting and our bean suppers. This Club helped me to learn to hug people, it was one of the "rules." They were posted in the office beside the door for all of us to read and obey. When we met someone at the door, we would have to hug hello instead of just shaking hands. I remember once getting the longest hug I think I ever had. Archie's sponsor hugged me until I hugged him back and meant it, he hung on. I learned after that. I had not been a hugger but now I can hug most people.

Right after I got home from work, I would change and go down to the Club. If no one was there at the time, there would be someone within the hour. Most of us went there after work to relax before going home to have supper. There were many arguments there, but each had to be resolved before we left. One time Archie had cleaned a motor boat, a job he was getting paid for, but the guy wasn't satisfied. I thought Archie did a good job and told the guy so. We got into an argument and I bought the boat—I didn't want it—and he sold me the boat—he didn't want to. Their sponsor came over to both of us and told us to quit acting like small children. End of argument. Of course, I didn't keep the boat and the guy took the boat home.

Archie's friend Barry had a house boat and it took me a lot of nerve to get on it. I was afraid of going into a boat if it was on the water. Eventually, I got sort of comfortable on the house boat but still couldn't get into a smaller boat. I was terrified of the water. Until I started writing this book, I didn't know why I was afraid of water. I had forgotten about the time I almost drowned in that swimming hole when I was a teenager. Now I know that is why I couldn't go on a boat. Archie wanted to go on a cruise but we never did because of my fear of water.

Learning who I am, I had to learn how to be myself. I had been trying to be someone else for so long. I knew what others wanted but I had no idea what I wanted. I knew what to do to help others but couldn't help myself until I got in the Program and they taught me to put the focus on me and I was lost at first. If someone asked me what I wanted to do, I had no idea, so I would ask back, "What do you want to do?" It took a long time of working on me and to this day it is a work in progress.

I also learned to trust others, and to get along with people while we were in that Club besides learning to hug and like/love people. It made the Program for me easier, besides going to meetings, we were living the Program like we were in an extended family. Then, I had to learn to do it with my own family at home.

Chapter 12
The Devil

I started smoking cigarettes when I was a teenager in high school, just to fit in, and continued until I became pregnant. I found it easy to quit that time, I didn't inhale it so I wasn't addicted to it. People told me that it would affect my baby. Not wanting to harm her in any way, I knew I was having a girl, I didn't smoke. I didn't start up again until after the youngest was at least six months old. To this day, I don't know what set me off to start again. I walked to the store, bought a package and from then on, I smoked. This time when I smoked, I inhaled. I was up to two and a half packages a day by the time I wanted to quit. Men at work would bum cigarettes from me and one day, because I had a cold, I started smoking menthol cigarettes—thinking that the menthol would help my cold.

When the men asked if I had a cigarette, I offered them a menthol and they said, "No thanks." So, I continued to smoke them. They never asked again. I became addicted to the menthol in the cigarettes. It took me two years to get off the menthol then. The next step was to quit completely. This time it wasn't so easy to quit.

Some of the firemen—Archie was a volunteer fireman—were quitting smoking. I had tried a few times, but failed so I said I would join them and try again. Because money had become my god, I wanted to save money so I quit. A carton of cigarettes would cost me $10 and I would buy a carton a week plus some individual packages. I could visualize the little money I had, going up in smoke. When the house next door, where we used to live, caught on fire I was the only one who didn't smoke. The firemen who had been quitting were smoking again by this point. However, this was too close of a call to one of their own, (meaning Archie). The house fire next door was so intense, it heated our house to the point of cracking our windows and pealing the paint on our house—a very close call. My reply to them was, "If I can do it, you can too."

Before the Program I had never heard of 'detachment'. Detachment does not mean to detach from the person but from their problems. I am not responsible for another person's disease or recovery from it. I can still love them but don't take on their responsibility to do what they need to do for themselves.

At first, I didn't understand that I needed to detach from the problem not the person. If I could separate the problem from the person, I could still love the person but hate the problem. OK, now to put it into practice. it's not as easy as it sounds; at least it wasn't for me. I remember an argument we had and I tried to detach from whatever it was we were fighting and yelling about at the time, no idea now, I found I had to get away from both the problem and the person. I used to call it 'amputation'. I went away for a while and when I came back, I was calmer and was able to handle it in a much better and calm way. We agreed to disagree and leave it alone. I did this, 'amputation' a few times before I was able to stay and face my husband and stay relatively calm. Now to do it with the next person. My oldest daughter, Annette, who was also an alcoholic and drug addict. She and I did not get along very well. We just couldn't see eye to eye.

Annette was in British Columbia when I was working on detachment and was finally able to let her go and started to look at her and treat her for who she was—a woman of her own—not MY daughter. She was my daughter but I found myself not thinking of her as a possession any longer. When she asked, on one of the times she called, what she should do, I asked her what she thought she should do. She said, "Mom, aren't you going to tell me what to do?" I replied, "No, you are grown up and you have to make your own decision. Besides, you are 2000 miles away. There is nothing I can do." She made the decision and things were OK for a while. Then she had to get out of there when things got really bad for her. Mom and I made arrangements to get her home. She came home in March 1991.

She moved back in with us and we became friends. I was then able to treat her as a daughter and a grown woman of her own. I found that she had learned a lot being out in the world on her own. We were able to go shopping together and she treated me by buying things for me like an independent person. It felt good to finally be a friend with my daughter. She joined the Program also and worked her program to the best of her abilities.

Archie and I were involved with the Programs quite a bit and we had a camp ground twelve step weekend that we helped organize and I was doing the kitchen which was opened for food to buy. Breakfast had to be ready to start at 7:00 a.m. and supper at about 5:00 p.m. with chips and drinks to sell in between. I bought, sold and cooked it all. Annette being home now was able to help and she did. She had been going to another meeting and knowing some the men from Harvest House Drug and Alcohol Rehabilitation she invited them to help at the camp. That weekend, I met some of the young men in the Program, some of the staff and on the last day, which was a Sunday, I also met the Director and Pastor of Harvest House. This was the start of a relationship with them that has lasted to this day. We were invited to their service but I never thought at the time that I would leave the Catholic Church we had been attending since birth. We were still going to church but instead of the breakfast meeting, we started to go to the service at Harvest House Ministries right after, missing the first part of the service.

By September Annette was diagnosed with acute lymphocytic leukemia. I went to the hospital three times a week on my own after work to visit her and once every Sunday after church with Archie. Parking about one mile away from the hospital on the street because it was free, I lost a lot of weight without thinking about it. That was about eight miles a week I walked. The following year in October 1992, Annette passed away but she was clean and sober for a little over a year. She was proud of that. So were we.

One night, after I drove one of the guys from Harvest House home from a meeting, he told me that I would leave the Catholic Church and start coming to Harvest House Ministries. As I was about to protest and say, "No, I won't." He said not to say anything because I didn't believe it right now but it would happen. That came true. I am glad that we do not know the future because of the way it all happened I don't think that I could have handled it at all.

We went to church the Sunday after Annette passed away and I came out of church so angry that I didn't want to go back there. When I had asked the priest to say a few words at the graveside he lit into me and said he wouldn't. He didn't agree that she was being cremated. He also said he didn't know me. Archie and I were Eucharistic Ministers and I was also a reader and helped him with the mass and he didn't know me? He also looked down on country people—he was from a very large city. My program went right out the window. Meaning I forgot everything I had learned. I forgot that I wasn't to take things personal. I got angry and stayed that way for quite a while. The next weekend we started going to Harvest House Ministries for church. On the day of the funeral, it was Harvest House who supported us, not the church we had been going to all our lives and helped every time we could, which was almost every weekend at times.

I started getting anxious and feeling really bad but didn't know what was happening. I finally found out that it was anxiety and panic attacks. I discovered that I couldn't be around many people at one time. If there were two or more people at a meeting I would leave, I couldn't stand it. I also quit drinking coffee after 12:00 noon so I could sleep at night. Eventually I was able to get out again and went for counselling.

I had read about deliverance and wandered about it. I wanted and needed to be delivered from many things so I talked to someone from Harvest House about it. He told me that Pastor Adam did deliverance but before I could go for it, I had to read a certain book. That book explained all about what deliverance is and what to expect. I was glad I read it before going. It was very enlightening and informative for me.

The day of my first appointment, I had a problem getting my car out of the drive way. It was stuck on the frozen ice and snow and with me trying to get out, the wheels spun in one place digging into the ice and it really got stuck. I remembered something that I read in the book and knew it was the devil trying to stop me. Being as stubborn as I was, I was not going to let him win. I called Harvest House and told them I would be there but would be late. I then went back out and put the car in reverse and then in forward and rocked the car until it eventually moved enough to get out of the drive way.

That day started my counselling and I had many appointments after that. I had several sessions later as well for different problems. Sometimes, if you get the right counsellor, you get healthier faster. I say, the right counsellor, because Archie and I had gone to a counsellor when he was drinking and that counsellor was not a good fit for either of us. It was marriage counselling and we found out after we quit going to her that she was going through a divorce herself. How can she counsel someone as to what to do when she can't handle her own marriage?

In 1993, I just couldn't take staying in the same house any longer. Every time I went to the washroom, I had to pass Annette's bedroom and it devastated me so much that I wanted out of that house. Archie and I talked about it and we decided to sell. We had tried before but it hadn't sold. This time I called my school friend, who was a real estate agent, and asked her if she would handle the sale. She said yes and I started to pack. The place was sold and we paid off our bills along with the existing mortgage and very little left for the buying of a new home. But we did have enough for a small down payment. I put my trust in God to make it all work out.

Having sold our home, we had to move out for the 1st of April but had no house to move into. In the early part of March, we went to an open house but didn't get it. Archie went out on Saturday to look around and then stopped in the restaurant next door, and overheard the real estate people who were in there. They were saying that there just wasn't any house for sale out there to be had. He came home really discouraged and worried. Somehow, I wasn't. I knew we would get a house by the 1st of April and move. I had been packed for months, ready to go. I was at peace with the idea of not having a house right then and there to move into because "I knew" that we would have one on time. I don't know how I knew, but I knew. The girls at work kept telling me to get going on finding a place, and my answer to them was "No worries, we'll have a place on time." I really believed that.

That Sunday morning on the way to church, we noticed a "for sale" sign that Archie said wasn't there on Saturday morning. I called my real estate agent friend and told her we wanted to see it. She told me that we couldn't afford it. I said, "Well, it won't hurt to see it anyways." We went, put in an offer and by the next weekend it was ours. God did come through for us. The people had to get a motel to live in until they could find a new place to live. We had our new home. In the first couple of weeks after we had moved in, Harvest House brought chairs and the church service was held in our back yard and our property was blessed that Sunday. This was the last place we were to live, retire and enjoy for the rest of our lives. For twenty-four years we both loved and enjoyed it and I had it for another two years before having to restart my life again elsewhere.

We had lots of flowers already growing both in the front yard and back yard come spring. The back yard had flowers on both ends of the deck and one a few feet beyond that. A crab apple tree grew in one corner of the lot that I made crab apple jelly from that first year and for a few years after that. There was no privacy in the back yard because there were not many trees until we planted a lot as the years went by. There was a circle of sumac trees at the back end of the house. It had a clear spot in the middle of the circle that became Archie's 'getaway' until it all had to be cut down because of the destruction of trees from a small tornado in the summer of 1997 (the same year as the ice storm). This was his way of getting privacy. And also sitting out of the sun.

He worked for hours in the garden which he planted beyond the crab apple tree at the backside of the lot. We ate fresh vegetables every summer until we were not able to keep it up any longer. Our backyard was like a show place for me. We had friends who used to come visit every summer when our garden was ready to pick and the raspberries which were later than the regular ones were also ready to pick. The raspberry patch was between the crab apple tree and the garden and we extended it until it hid the garden from the house.

The front yard had nice, small yellow flowers along the front of the house from the garage to the front door and some small trees beyond that. Those flowers were cut down one Saturday morning as Archie was cutting the grass and he spotted a snake. He was terrified of snakes. He ran all the flowers down as he went after the snake to kill it with the riding lawn mower. He got the snake and the whole nest of them. The flowers never grew again.

When we first moved in, the ditches were very deep and was always full of water. This is where the snakes came from. They came because of the swampy water in the ditch. A petition was passed around to have the ditch cleaned out and culverts put in to get rid of the water. Finally, it was done and we were able to cut the grass in the ditch until the new youth centre opened in the old fire hall on the main street and they built a septic in the small park two doors down from us. For about two years our ditch was good but a truck went into the park through the ditch and broke the culvert there. After that we had oily and dirty water in the ditch. This was our introduction to now being in a city instead of a small village in a township. We tried to get it repaired but only got promises, nothing was done.

Along both sides of the drive, Archie made more flower beds and we planted flowers there every spring and he also planted his peonies in different places around the front and back yards and he also planted lilacs. We had brought them from the previous home. I was able to help him with the flower beds back then and they were very clean from weeds because of the two of us working at them. I was no longer pulling weeds as I had before in pulling hair when I was angry. I was now past dealing with anger in that way.

I was proud of our yard; it was one of the only ones with flowers on our street. Only the lady next door had a small flower bed but no one else. To anyone looking for our place I would say "the second on the right with the flowers." They could find our place without any problem.

It was on a quiet street and a much newer and nicer house than the one we had on the main street. It had three bedrooms, a family room downstairs and an unfinished room that had been used as a workshop. Archie and his friend, Barry built me book shelves on two of the walls from floor to ceiling and painted the rest. I filled those shelves with books of all kinds. Craft books, cook books, recovery books of different things, novels and Christian novels, Children's books and a set of encyclopedias, which I had bought to help the girls while they were in school.

We made the family room that was downstairs into a living room with the TV, a couch, a coffee table and chairs for visitors. We used it for gatherings and our Christmas tree was usually down there. Except in the summer time, we would have the gatherings out in the backyard. The basement living room had a wood stove and in winter was very warm. This is the room we used the most often. When we first moved in, I bought new furniture for the living room on the main floor and made it into a show room (someone else's name for it). No kids were allowed in it. I didn't want it to get ruined. It was quite a few years before I let anyone in there except to look at it. I really was obsessed with the living room looking good. Now looking back, I don't know why because I no longer have it, except the couch and one lamp from it. I either sold or gave everything else away.

Then I found out that I was allergic to book mites and had to get rid of most of my books. Doctor's orders. That was the hardest thing for me to do. I treasured those books as I treasured everything I had. I got rid of a lot but I didn't get rid of all of them though. I just couldn't do it. It wasn't until after I was living in a very small apartment that I got rid of some more. This is the room that I filled up, and I mean filled up, with craft supplies, either bought and/or saved from recycled items to make crafts. Those shelves which used to be full of books were now filled with craft supplies and whatever I thought I might need in the future.

Chapter 13
Operation

I was shopping at a craft store one day and as I was looking around at the finished crafts at the back of the store, I noticed a lady doing a craft. She was doing one that I was making at home at the time. I could see that she wasn't going to succeed because she was doing it wrong. I told her what she needed to do, she did it, and it worked out for her. She had never done it before. She asked me if I would go and teach. I said "Yes" and was half way home before I realized what I had done. I was retired from work but now I had committed myself to do something during the day. I taught the craft she was trying to do plus eventually two other crafts as well. I was surprised with a five-year gift for keeping that job for that long. I taught these crafts until I needed an operation on for my throat. I had wanted to teach but it took forty years for it to happen and I did get to do it. God's timing is not my timing.

We went through hard times financially and other things for a few years here as Archie wasn't working and I couldn't. I had retired medically. Someone mentioned that maybe we should sell the house and get something smaller but my answer to that was, "God gave us this house, He won't let us loose it." And He didn't.

In the fall of 1997, the ice storm hit. We had freezing rain and it froze on everything, making everything really heavy. The wires and anything that couldn't take the weight, collapsed. No one had electricity and, in some parts, no telephone. No one had heat and we couldn't get gas in the area. The army got called in to help. We were one of the lucky ones. We had a wood stove to keep warm and a battery radio to hear the news. Our basement had already flooded but the electricity had come back on long enough to clear it and then it went out for two or three weeks more. When the sump-pump hole would get full, Archie would pump it out with a gas pump, which we borrowed. Putting the hose through the basement window to reach the sub-pump hole for the water to go out into the front yard. Two friends moved in with their dog and when their telephone went out their son showed up at the door with his camping gear to sleep on our living room floor. Mom and her new husband came to stay one night but went back home because they said my house was like a zoo and they couldn't stay any longer. One night was enough. We spent the time cooking as much of the food as we could from the freezer on the wood stove. The rest spoiled. I went out only one night during that time but Archie and a friend went door to door pumping out basements and to help wherever they could.

Archie loved to cook and so he took over cooking supper every night. When he was home, he would cook breakfast and lunch as well. I still didn't like to be in the kitchen doing housework so I let him do it. Because of my medical problems I would cough with the smell of the food cooking. I guess he didn't want my germs in the food so he did it. Eventually he did all the cooking. Once in a while, I would cook if I had to but not often.

In December 2001, Archie had an appointment at the doctor's office and while he was there, he had a heart attack. That was scary for me. I thought I would lose him then. On New Year's Eve, while I was at a party and celebrating because he was on the mend, he had another one while in the hospital. He needed an angioplasty and stents. I had to do all the driving because the doctor made him promise not to drive for five months. Here I was again, doing all the driving because he couldn't. When he lost his licence to drive during the drinking years, I resented it. It was his fault. At least this time it was different. I knew it wasn't his fault. I was doing it but not resenting it. He did heal to lead a normal life as if he had never had a heart attack.

One priest we had, told us one day that if we were not being fed in the church we were attending, we were to go elsewhere. He meant that we were to go to a spiritual church. Leaving the Catholic Church for us to go to Harvest House Ministries was the spiritual place to go. I have grown faster spiritually since then. I started reading the Bible at a "Life in the Spirit" seminar that we took in the Catholic Church and continued to read here also. The difference was that it was now explained why I had to do things and what it all meant. Knowing the difference is so uplifting and I wanted more. We got into Bible studies and learned together. Since Archie had problems with reading, I read the Bible/Bible study questions and books out loud to him and wrote down his answers as well as my own. I would read while he made supper or he would sit there and listen.

One day I said, "You must be getting tired of hearing me."

And he replied, "No, I like the sound of your voice."

I will never forget him saying that. It blessed me so much. This was such a big change in him and in me. We now could stand each other and work with each other without fighting and even like to listen to each other. We had both come a long way. Even now, thinking of that night and him saying that, I am tearing up.

One of the Bible studies we took was "The Bait of Satan" by John Bevere. It is all about taking the bait of offence. I had been learning to forgive through the Program and then through what I was learning at church but this book helped me to *want* to forgive. There was one person I wasn't willing to completely forgive but doing the exercise in this book helped me to completely forgive her. What a freeing feeling and experience. That was a few years ago and now I can converse with her and not feel anger towards her. The only reason I did the exercise was because I had to show that I fully did the study to get a certificate. The certificate didn't come—don't know why—but the reward I got was the total forgiveness and freedom I received.

As I already said, I was coughing and choking, by now almost constantly, and was sent to all kinds of doctors to see what was wrong. This went on for years. I was sent to an ears, nose and throat specialist at the hospital by my family doctor, but when the Health and Welfare Department doctor called him, he became offended and said that he wouldn't see me any more since I had gone to another doctor. I was later referred to another ears, nose and throat doctor in the same office. This time after two appointments that specialist told me that he knew what needed to be done. He said I had a choice.

1. Fix my voice box but I wouldn't be able to breathe,
2. Fix my throat but I wouldn't be able to talk,
3. Or both and I could breathe and talk.

It meant an operation to put in a trachea. That day was one of my scariest days of my whole life. The first two were not really choices, so I had to take the third one. I asked to think about it and he told me not to think too long on it because my throat was closing more and more and soon wouldn't be able to breathe at all and I would die.

Since it cost money to park the car, I had my husband take my car and park elsewhere until I was ready to go, then I would call him. All I could think of was that the doctor was going to cut my throat. I called my husband and when he got out of the car for me to get into the driver's seat, I broke down and told him that the doctor wanted to slit my throat. He asked what he could do and I told him to take me to see Pastor Adam. When we got there, I explained what the doctor had said, crying the whole time. After I was finished, he said, "What do you want me to do? Tell you what to do?" and I just cried "Yes!" As soon as he said, "Well get it done." I felt relieved and calmed right down. I believe God had spoken to me through Pastor Adam. I was no longer afraid and was calm the whole time until it was all over. I called the doctor and on July 2nd 2003, our 37th wedding anniversary, the operation was done. The doctor told me that it was a temporary thing. To this day I still have it.

Archie was asked to put on a class at Harvest House at night. At first, he was very nervous and didn't want to go because he felt very inadequate but as time went on, he enjoyed it and felt good about what he was doing and felt much better about himself. He was happy that he was making a difference in these boys' lives. He shared himself with them. I also tried in the "phone room" making phone calls for donations. I wasn't very good at it. I quit. If I had continued, I might have gotten better but I didn't give it a good chance.

After a few years, I decided to volunteer but this time as a verifier, verifying the particulars of the donors, so we could send a tax receipt. This worked better until I needed cataract surgery on my eyes and couldn't see enough to verify. I did other paper work until one night I quit. I had a disagreement with the leader in the phone room at that time. While I was there, I learned a lot of what Harvest House was all about. I knew a lot before, but now learned more from the inside. I was able to talk to the guys, to find out what they were like, what the Program was doing for them and what they wanted in life.

When I had an appointment to get my eyes checked and measured for the operation it took two nurses to hold my eye open to put the drops in. Before the operation I couldn't go near my eyes without closing them. I was surprised after the operation how easy it was. I was so scared going in that my blood pressure went up and I had to wait until it came down before they did anything. The hardest part was all the drops they had to put in. The operation itself was a breeze. I was put asleep and it didn't hurt. I had to wear a metal eye patch to stop me from scratching my eye while it was healing. When I went for my second eye a few months later, I found it much easier and was not scared. It made a difference because I knew what to expect this time. Also, after each operation I had to put eye drops in every day and tried having my husband do it for me but my eyes kept closing when he got near my eyes; I found that I was able to do it myself.

Harvest House is a Drug and Alcohol Rehabilitation opened in 1979 by our Pastor Adam that takes in drug addicts and alcoholics in to help with their rehabilitation to become productive individuals before they go into society to live their lives clean and sober. Some come from the streets, and some from jail but they learn to leave all that behind—if they follow the Program. They must attend church, Harvest House Ministries—which I am a member of, to obtain faith in Jesus Christ. Here, they learn ways to live a good life, get an education, how to work and do things they have never learned (because of their addictions).

When my step dad died in 2013, I didn't know what my mother was going through, I found out later, but it was too late to help my mom go through it. She found her husband sitting on his chair, he got as a Christmas present, and thought he was sleeping but when she touched him, he was cold. I thought, "Hope to never be in that position ever." Less than four years later I was to find out that I would be in the almost the same situation. As the executor, I was called immediately by the next-door neighbour.

My brothers Arthur and Oscar thought it better to sell her house and get rid of everything in it. She was put in an old age home. I was the executor but because Mom was in the beginning of dementia my brother, Oscar took her to her lawyer and changed the executor and power of attorney to him and a friend of Mom's. Mom had changed it to name my brother Arthur and I quite a few years previous because she didn't trust Oscar to do what she really wanted. She also didn't trust her friend completely. As a confident, she would tell me often of not trusting either of them even though she loved them. So I, nor my youngest brother Jimmy, had any say in anything. We were the ones who had taken care of Mom when she needed it, and drove her to her appointments and went running when she needed something. My mom wanted to stay in her home, but they really didn't care. They thought they knew what was better for her. She lasted only six months after her husband had passed. I believe she died of a broken heart. She lost her will to live.

I was devastated. I just didn't seem to get me together to do anything. I lost interest in everything. Part of me was gone. Every time something happened that I once would have called my mom to tell her about, I knew now I couldn't and that she would never be there for me to call ever again. Every Sunday, after church Archie and I would go visit her. That was our Sunday afternoons for years. My mom and I had become the best of friends and were able to talk about everything and anything. As I changed, I realized that I needed someone who knew me as well as she did that no matter what I did or said she would still love me. She was my mom. If only I could have done that with my own daughter. Coming near Christmas that year, I didn't want anything to do with it. Someone told me about the one-day bereavement session about "getting through Christmas while grieving." I went and it did help me a lot. They told us that we needed to keep traditions the same as much as we could and to celebrate Christmas but on a smaller scale. Christmas Eve, Archie and I went to the same church as we always brought Mom to for midnight mass. Since no one else came—Brother Jimmy, sister-in-law Angela, step dad, and Aunt May—we were alone in that pew. Both of us felt the pain of losing my mother. The following year we went elsewhere.

Mom had become more than my mother and friend. She was my hairdresser as well. She and I would do each other's hair. When I used to dye my hair, back when I was working and had long hair, she would do it for me. She also did home perms. She showed me how to perm her hair and how to cut it. When it got too hard for me to look after my hair, like washing it, I decided to have it cut really short. Mom braided it and cut the braid off. She cut it so short at the back that I could not grab it with my fingers. She continued to do my hair until we were both not able to do it. She then went to a hairdresser. I started cutting my own hair. Every time I went to a hairdresser, I found they didn't cut it the way I wanted it. I really missed the closeness we had when we were doing each other's hair.

When a mother of a friend passed away, I was able to be there for her and we talked about it and how I felt when my mom passed and what I did or didn't do. Just being there for her, also helped me to heal more. I would not have been able to be there for her the same way if I had not gone through the same thing. No one can really know how someone feels if they never experienced it. They may think they know but they don't. "I know how you feel" comments at the funeral parlour seems to be what a lot of people say but they don't know, if they have never been through it. It is better to say nothing or just ask how we are doing instead.

After my mother passed away, and seeing all the work we had to do to get rid of some of my mother's things I decided to start getting rid of some of mine also. I didn't want anyone to have the same problem. I started with the things in my craft room and my craft supplies. One night at one of our dances, I heard a lady telling her friends that she had sold her house to move to a senior's apartment and had to get rid of all her craft stuff. I went over to talk to her and asked her how and where did she get rid of it all. She told me that schools can use it. So, I filled up a few boxes and brought to the public school near my home. I made that trip once more but I wanted to spread it out more.

Talking to a friend from Harvest House, I found out that one of the wives worked at a day care. As it turned out, their son went to another day care and she also had a friend who worked at another day care. She would take everything and distribute it all for me. The first trip they did was a car load, but the next trip was a truck load. I was finally able to see the floor in that room—a little bit. Letting stuff go was so hard for me. I would do only a little at a time, I just couldn't handle more than that. As I decluttered, I found that I was also decluttering my brain. By that, I mean I found myself being able to think better and not getting 'lost' in so many things or thoughts. It gave me hope to continue to get rid of things I never used and was keeping 'just in case'. I continued to declutter for another few years.

Then my husband passed away. Now I had his things and the rest of mine to get rid of. I knew I had to do it but it was still hard. For the first two years after his passing, I held garage sales, had ads on line in different places to sell and give away our things. I also found an on-line auction sale that would take care of the auction of my things right from my house without taking anything out of it. It cost a certain amount and a percentage of sales but they came in and took pictures of everything, catalogued it all, took care of their web site auction of my things, took the bids and at the end came back to my house and took care of the removing of the sold items, making sure that the right people were picking up what they had paid for. I really didn't make much money from it but I did get rid of a lot of things. What didn't sell, I was left with. I continued selling and giving things away until I sold and moved out of my home. It did get a little easier to get rid of things as time went on.

Today, once I decide to get rid of something, it's no problem. God has changed my whole way of thinking. I am free of most of my possessions and can let them go easily.

Chapter 14
Never Woke Up

In 2016, we celebrated our fiftieth wedding anniversary. This time we said our own vows. The difference is I knew I loved him the way I should have felt about him when we got married fifty years before. It was a small ceremony at Harvest House with our paster and friend, Paster Adam. Only a few friends, real friends, attended. There was no reception this time. I wanted one but was talked out of it. I was reminded that we really did not have the money to pay for one and really didn't need one. I agreed. I enjoyed it much better than the first time because it wasn't just a ceremony but a profession of our love for each other.

Archie was still working at seventy-three years old. He always said that he would work until the day he died. He retired, but while cutting our widowed neighbours' grass, we got a call to see if he wanted a job. He took that job doing yard maintenance. He made a much better wage and had responsibilities there that were never in his other jobs. He loved working there. Since he now had more money than I did, I took advantage and was able to let him be the "man" he always wanted to be. The "bread earner and husband looking after his wife." The more I would let him do it the more he was happy about it. This made life happier at home also. I felt good to be able to help him finally. He would joke about it to others but at home; I saw the difference and how he revelled in "taking care of me" financially and otherwise. Sometimes it made me feel like I was no good for him but knew that I was doing the right thing by him. One day my sister-in-law, Angela said she was a "kept woman" and I replied that "in that case, I'm a kept woman too." She had stated that her husband was working, bringing in the money and then coming home to cook supper. Archie was doing all that and more.

He would work from the springtime until late into the fall and then be off for the winter. For me, it became a rollercoaster of getting used to having him at home in the winter, then not for the summer months. I found myself being able to do whatever and whenever I wanted to while he was at work without having to take his presence into consideration. Then, he was home again and things changed. I found I couldn't do something without expecting to be interrupted by him wanting to ask a question, talk or go somewhere. By the time I was used to having him at home—and I did like having him around—off to work he would go again for the summer. This went on for a few years. I really never got used to it. When he was home, he made lunch and expected me to eat it. I never eat lunch. I have a late breakfast and then supper. I was always trying to watch my weight because of the amount of food he would put in my plate. I tried to have him give me less but he would complain that I wasn't eating enough. The problem was that I usually would not leave any food in my plate, I would eat it all. It was so good. He was a good cook. He was trying so hard to be good to me.

When we first met my friends Giselle and Pierre we were accepted and welcomed like one of them. They are social drinkers but we didn't drink, they didn't go to church but we did, they are not in recovery and we both were. It didn't make any difference to them. I wasn't used to be treated as an equal, loved, and included. We still have those differences. I am so blessed to have them in my life today.

In 2016, Giselle and Pierre wanted to go to Cuba but we couldn't see spending that much money to go in a plane to anywhere. We decided to go to British Columbia again, this time to visit Archie's cousin. Then a friend had a heart attack and died. Archie said, "Maybe we should go to Cuba, we may never get the chance to go again." We called our friends and said we would go with them. Today, I am glad that we did. We went in February 2017 and in May he passed away. He never got the chance again as he said. I did go back the following three years. We had made friends there and I am in contact with most of them on the computer now. It was hard for me to go on a holiday without him but with our friends with me, we could talk about him and I did make it through. I knew they were missing him also. When I went back that first year without Archie, I told one of the waitresses and she teared up. She remembered him, they used to tease him, as he teased them with "Shaky, Shaky."

He liked to make people smile and be happy. He did it quite often and seemed to enjoy doing it. I thought he didn't know when to quit once he started. I would get angry with him when he continued on and on. I never thought that I would ever miss it, but I do. When we were travelling in our friends' truck, the men would be in the front seat and we women in the back seat. That way we could talk, man to man, and woman to woman. When Pierre would ask, "Anything coming?" Archie would say "A flocks of turtles" which meant nothing was coming. It became a norm for us to hear it and know what he meant. He knew it made us smile.

The company sold out and he was let go. In May 2017, while we were away, he got a call and was asked if he could work another summer. He was to go in to talk about it to the boss on Tuesday since Monday was a holiday. It turns out that he worked that day and came home really tired. After supper, he started the dishes and I told him to leave them, that I could do it the next day. I convinced him to relax and we could go downstairs and watch TV.

He went to sleep while we were watching TV and never woke up. I looked over and he was sleeping. Knowing that he was tired, I let him sleep, but the next time I looked over I knew he was gone. That night will be etched in my mind the rest of my life. Somehow, I called 911 and when I called our best friends, Giselle and Pierre, the phone was taken from me by a policeman who took it from my hands and went outside to speak to my friends. They came over immediately—they lived an hour away—but the police never left until they got to my house and he spoke to them. A policeman or fireman, someone in uniform, kept asking me if there wasn't anyone closer that I could call. I told them that family lived closer but they wouldn't come. I called Pastor Adam, our friend, and told him that Archie was gone. We went to the hospital and they had him on machines to breathe for him. I said goodbye to him then. We left after they disconnected him and the next few days are a blur.

For the next few days, Giselle and Pierre took me to the restaurant to make sure I ate. For weeks afterwards, I would get phone calls from them and other close friends asking, “Did you eat today?” or “What did you eat today?” to make sure I ate. Sometimes I would eat just so I could answer them, “Yes” and be able to answer what I ate. Knowing that they really cared got me through those weeks and months. His male friends also helped me when I needed help, like cutting the grass, cleaning the driveway of snow in the winter or whatever was needed outside. It got me through that first year. People from our church continued to help and are still helping me today. Without God and my friends, I don't know what I would have done. I am so grateful for God and them in my life.

When I was listening to the radio, I noticed that I was really hearing the words being sung not just the music. I took solace in them. Some songs were so true to life and it seemed had been written just for me and my situation. They made me cry when I heard them, but that was part of me healing. One song I heard about a year after is *It's just sad* by Flatt Lonesome. It helped me to be OK even if I was sad and missing him.

One afternoon, I was sitting at the table feeling lonely, sad and really alone, and as I do many times, talking to myself.

I asked myself, “What would I changed if I could?”

“I want Archie back,” I answered.

I thought for a moment and then out of my own month came. “No, I wouldn't, I couldn't do that to him. I love him too much to have him come back to this crazy world. He is much better off than I am."

A peace came over me and I felt much better. The loneliness and feeling alone left. Still felt sad but that was it was OK. He is in heaven and being brought back on this earth would be really cruel to him. As much as I miss him, I realized that he had gone through hell on this earth and had paid his dues—to be in heaven with Jesus, his mother and father, his sister and Annette was a much better place to be. That peace that I got that day is still with me today. I believe that Jesus has given me that peace beyond all understanding and it has made life easier for me. Knowing that He is here with me at all times and will get me through whatever I need to do.

All my life until I got into the Program, I felt lonely even in a crowd. I grew up in a large family but still felt lonely. It didn't make sense to me. How could I feel lonely when I wasn't alone? But I did feel alone most of the time. I somehow didn't feel like I belonged. I remember, many times, after a run in with my dad that I would go up to my bedroom and write a letter to "Whoever" and would start with, "I know I must be adopted because he can't be my father the way he treats me." Don't remember what else I used to write but the first of that letter, written many times, reminds me how I felt then. It was years later that I learned why I felt that way. In counselling with my pastor, I learned that my mom was raped by my dad and I was born from that. He was my dad.

I no longer feel alone. I am never alone. I have Jesus with me at all times. When I feel I need to have a physical person to talk to, I can call someone or go visit.

We used to be members of an Ole Tyme Fiddlers Club in our town and there we met our musician friends. We didn't play but enjoyed the music and danced. Eventually, we got on the committee and got more involved. When the group in our town closed down Archie bought the set of drums and set them up at home. One day while we were with our friends shopping in a music store, he bought another set and set it up in our friends' house. When they would practice, he played and I felt left out. I picked up the tambourine and started playing with it. Since I don't know keys in music, I figured it would be the easiest to learn. NOT. To keep the beat, at first, wasn't easy for me. I had to practice and practice to learn how to keep the beat, when to play it and when not to, depending on who was singing, and what the song was. We practised at our friends Pierre and Giselle's home every Friday night for hours. After about a year, I decided to check on line to see if I was playing it right and found out that I was not. Eventually, I was able to develop my own style of playing it.

My girlfriend, Giselle bought me my first good tambourine. I had no intention on playing with the band outside of the practice. I was doing it to belong and for fun. Since Giselle bought me the tambourine I couldn't say no when she said I would be playing with them on stage. So that is what I did, joined them to play for other people. We played at the Old Time Music Clubs and other places around the area. We still only play for fun, there is no money in it. We play for charities like the pig roast in the summer and other things like birthdays and special occasions. Right now, because of the pandemic I haven't played for over a year. I really miss that.

When Archie passed away, I figured that I would quit playing but I got a phone call one day from someone who had her own band. She told me that when her husband died and she was first learning to play and sing, music was soothing and helped her through her grief. My friends called to tell me that we were to play at the Canada Day Celebration in a park. I went. I felt out of place, listening for the drums and really missing Archie, but I got through it. I played in other places and after a while I found that what she said was true. Playing had been soothing even though I missed Archie while I was up there on stage.

From an early age I loved country music and when I was in my teens Rock and Roll came out and I liked it too. There were groups from the city that used to play on the radio every lunch hour, and when we came home for lunch from school, when we lived across the field from it, we would listen to them. Now, I still listen to classic country (the country I grew up with) not today's country and Bluegrass and Gospel music. Lately, it's been more Bluegrass and Gospel than anything else. I find that it is more spiritual than other music. That's only my opinion, of course.

In 2019, we had been booked to visit Cuba; when the hurricane hit, it was cancelled so we booked for Jamaica and went there. Then Cuba was OK to receive people so we booked there also. We saw the devastation the hurricane had done in parts of Cuba, especially Cayo Coco, which is an independant island connected to the main island by a causeway. We saw part of that devastation as we left the airport and more when we got to the resort. We also saw that the resort had done the best they could to get back on their feet and had it looking good for us. Some of the resort rooms were never opened but those that were, were good. A lot of people complained, we were grateful that we were able to come back and things were good for us. Since we only ate our meals in the buffet restaurant, we didn't really miss the others on the resort. One restaurant was completely gone into the ocean, all that was left was the debris at the edge and a slab of cement that had been its foundation. The lobby was freshly painted and tidied up and it looked good to us. The beach was still the best.

I liked Jamaica but prefer the beach and the people in Cayo Coco, Cuba. The beach here was very small and the sand wasn't near as nice as Cuba. I didn't enjoy the entertainment as much as in Cuba. I found the food really good though. The people were also friendly and good to us. I did enjoy being there and I know now, that comparing it to Cuba was a mistake, I could have maybe enjoyed it more if I hadn't. We went on an excursion to see a plantation. We learned that there were many kinds of pineapples and even got to taste some. There was quite a bit of walking but I made it.

Back home in Canada, I kept the house as long as I could, but not being able to look after it, the trees got out of hand, and the flower beds became overgrown. By 2019, I decided that it was time. I would have to leave our home and move. I worked hard to sell and give away a lot of things that I didn't really want to see go but I felt I had no choice if I was to move into a smaller apartment. I just wasn't able to look after what God had given us the way he would have me do. I do miss sitting on the back deck or at the patio door looking out and seeing the birds, humming birds, chipmunks, black, brown and red squirrels and rabbits. Sometimes there would be a deer or two, or other small creatures.

We went back to Cuba in 2020 and while we were there Covid-19 hit the world. Things changed everywhere. When we got back in early March, we weren't required to quarantine, but shortly after, people who travelled or went out in public had to stay at least two metres away from each other and to wear a mask. “Stay at home” became the norm. Anyone who travelled had to quarantine for fourteen days. We also were told to wash our hands frequently. No more large gatherings and only certain number of people were permitted inside as well as outside. The colour of your area, indicating the level of risk of contracting the disease, determined how many people were allowed to get together. This included all holidays like Christmas, Easter, Canada Day and so on. There were fines handed out if you did not comply. A lot of people died, mostly in old age homes. Because I am more susceptible to get Covid I have to stay away from people which means no visitors or going out like I used to. Eventually they came out with a vaccine and we had to have two shots to be covered. I had both shots.

In my early years, I was so impatient that when I had to wait on something or someone I would fidget and say all kinds of unkind things against whatever or whoever was holding me up, it wasn't pretty. This is where my anger would show its ugly head. Even if I didn't say anything, people knew I was impatient by the way my body language would shout it out. In a line up at the store, I used to be like that, but now am more tolerant. The teller may be just learning and it is taking longer to do her job, or a customer has a complaint with the teller or something in the store and that has to be dealt with. I remember when I was that customer, not once but quite a few times, and held up the line. Now, I look at the delay as an opportunity to talk to people in the lineup and the time seems to go faster. The teller wouldn't get so nervous if she heard a word or two of encouragement instead of anger and impatience. When I am in a hurry, I still tend to be a little impatient until I remember that if I had started earlier, I wouldn't be in a hurry. It is no one else's fault if I didn't do what I was supposed to do in the first place. Of course, I am almost never in a hurry now like I was back in the day.

People would often say to me "you have such patience" when they saw me doing a jigsaw puzzle. I didn't, and still think it doesn't take any patience to do a jigsaw puzzle.

When we were first in the Program, Archie and his friend, Barry, decided to go away for a week together and I was left at home with the girls. All that week, I worked on acceptance. If I was to stay with him, I would have to accept him for the way he is, not the way I want him to be. Whatever he did that I didn't like or whatever he did not do that I didn't like I would have to accept. If I couldn't do that then I was going to have to leave him. That I didn't want to do so I had to learn to accept him. I decided to accept everything about him and stay with this man that I married.

When he came home, he wanted to talk. We went in the backyard on the back steps to talk. First thing he said was, "I don't want to be married any more. I want a friend." I was shocked and said, "You want a friend, go find a friend. I spent all week working out if I wanted to stay with you or not and I decided to accept you the way you are and stay. Now you want to not stay married?" and went into the house. For years I found it hard to accept certain things at times, but I stayed. Now I am glad I did. Archie and I had become the best of friends before he passed away. He got what he wanted and I found that I did want that also. Years later, we laughed about that conversation.

Another time that it was important to me was when I decided to make Pastor Adam my spiritual advisor. This means that I needed to accept what he says and to do what he says. I am also getting better in taking constructive instructions from him and not taking it as criticism. I know what he says is from God speaking through him. By doing that, I have been able to learn a lot more about myself and change for the better. There are still times he tells me something and I immediately do not agree but afterwards look at it and find that again he is right. This re-affirms that God has spoken through him to help me.

There are times that things are not acceptable to me, like being treated badly; putting myself in danger; being disrespected; any type of abuse to name but a few of them. Some things may be acceptable to some people but not to others. Some I may not like, but they are still acceptable, just not nice in my opinion.

Chapter 15

Follow God

Growing up, I had a few friends but as I now know, they were not true friends. Of course, I wasn't one either. I didn't know how to be a friend. I tested one friend to see if she would tell someone else what I told her one day. I was in high school and I told her something that was not true. That way when it got back to me, I would know that it was her who had told someone else. The next day, someone else told this story about me. She wouldn't tell me who told her but because I had told no one else, I already knew. I confronted my *friend* and told her she couldn't be my friend any longer because I had asked her to not repeat what I said and she had repeated it anyway. Today I have a few true friends. I know I can say anything to them and they will not repeat it, without me having to ask them not to. I also do the same. I had to learn to get along with people before I could be a friend. To have friends, you have to be a friend. It is a two-way street. I also had to learn about confidentiality and what it is.

I have worked against gossiping. I have gotten into trouble with some of my friends when I confront them about it. I find it too easy to join in gossip somehow and I don't like it. I work on it and I am OK for a while but then without thinking I find myself doing it. I remember twice I went to the person that was being gossiped about and asked if it was true. I also told them what was being said. Once was at work when a girl was being friendly with a guy. They were very good friends and that was it. She was married. After a while she was divorced and then they started going out. She came to me and told me that they were now involved and they could gossip all they wanted. Another time, it was with my musician friend. I told her that she was being talked about and told her what was being said. I didn't tell her who said it but she went to my friend and accused them of saying it. My friend was really angry but the gossiping stopped, at least around me. Some people don't seem to understand that you can be friends with the opposite sex without having an affair with them. Sometimes I wonder if there was gossip about Archie and I since we both had close friends of the opposite sex. I think the world would be awfully small if we couldn't be friends with others besides our own sex.

Also, I grew up thinking I had to take and take—clothing, food, whatever I wanted, not necessarily needed—if it was given freely. I may not have been in the position back then to give but there is more to taking and giving than tangible things. Today, I am more in a position to give than to take. I do need help (still hard for me to ask for it) but can and do give more. "*It is more blessed to give than to receive." Acts 20:35* I have found that this line from the Bible is true. The more I give, the more I get back in other ways. The more I am happy and content.

The more I had, the more I wanted. I would watch someone eat and if there was some food still in the bowls on the table, I would hurry to eat mine before someone else would take more. Afraid that they would have more than me. It was the same with everything. I had seen my mother go without so often, as we sat down at the table to eat, because there wasn't enough to go around. She would—all of a sudden—not be hungry or didn't want that last piece of whatever. I was afraid of going without so I didn't think twice in taking the last one even if someone else wanted it. That is not the way I was raised. I had learned to share but went without so many times after I was married that it became ingrained in me somehow to be greedy. I had to relearn all over again to share.

Tithing is one of the ways I give. The word tithing or 10% is in the Bible thirty-three times and says I am to give back to God only 10% that he gave me. I am allowed to keep 90%.

That's a good deal. At first, I gave, I felt I had to, not because I wanted to. Now, I give because I want to. I know that when I do, God will give me whatever I need in abundance. It has happened over and over since I started to give freely. When I get any amount of money now, I take out the first 10% to pay back to God. He does look after me much better than I can do myself. I didn't have any extra money before I started to tithe and because of that, I felt I couldn't afford it. Now, I know I can't afford not to. Money will come from directions I could never have dreamed of. In my head, it doesn't make sense but that is the way I find it to be. So, you see I can't afford to not to give. God has blessed me abundantly in every possible way because I put Him first in my life. This may sound like preaching, but I am telling it the way it is with me today. Without Him I am nothing and can do nothing. I know that and when I forget it—and at times I still do—things don't go so well for me.

When we got married, I also became instantly in debt. Archie believed that if you want to own something you must go into debt to do it. I didn't, but I found that I seemed to always be in debt from then on. I refused to get a credit card for a very long time and managed to do that until we bought our first house. Now we were in debt because we had a mortgage and eventually, I was talked into getting a mortgage line of credit at the bank. I needed a car and used it, Archie needed to renew his car insurance and used it. It went on from there. I got a credit card but was able to keep it in check. Archie's credit card went to the limit a few times and by the time renewal of the mortgage came he paid it off by putting it on the mortgage renewal, raising the amount of the mortgage. We have been lucky that the bank was able to give us a lower monthly payment that we could afford. I learned to be more and more frugal with my money and we were able to live that way. There were many nights that I couldn't sleep because of owing money. I worried on not being able to pay the payments and still get food and other bills paid for. By the time Archie passed away we owed more on the mortgage than we did when we bought the house and owed the mortgage line of credit also.

I recycled whatever I could throughout the years. Some people thought that I should throw out most of the things I kept, but I couldn't do it. I used and reused most of it. If I couldn't use it the way it was, I would cut it up and make something else from it. Pop can tabs were used for the back of pictures to hang on the wall, used wrapping paper and tissue paper were used in decoupage items, pictures from magazines and calendars were used for a lot of things, cans as covered containers, and buttons for earrings and pins. These are just a few of the items I made out of recycled things and sold to make extra money to get by.

When I found I couldn't keep the house because of not being able keep the inside clean and in good repair, looking after the yard properly, and watching it grow like a wild property with the trees overgrown and some dead ones, etc., I decided to sell it. The first thing I did was to pay all my debts off and buy a new car. My smart car needed too much repairs and it was coming on ten years old so I decided to buy new instead of repairing it. The salesman was surprised when I said I was paying cash for it. I am now living debt free finally. I still have bills like heating, electricity, telephone and cell phone but that is to be expected. I can sleep with these needs in my life.

In this pandemic, we are not to touch each other and are not to get too close to each other; we must wear a mask in public, or with someone outside your home and, in my case, when I am in the hall of the building I live in. Not having touched anyone in over a year, I was afraid that when I would be allowed to do so I wouldn't be able to do it. It took a lot of changing to be able to hug someone and now I was afraid that I would have to learn all over again. I am depending on God to get me through this. As I am working at getting this book ready for the editors, I have had some times to get out and to actually hug people. My fears are hopefully behind me. I can hug again.

My left knee started being sore at first. Then it got worse. When it was held in one position for any length of time and then moved it was stiff and painful. I found it hard to find a position to put it in so I could sleep at night and found it very painful when moving it while I walked.

The doctor had sent me for an ex-ray on it and said that it was arthritis but I knew it wasn't arthritic pain. I have had arthritic pain before when I had rheumatoid arthritis. I got prayer for it. It seemed to get better for a little while, but the pain came back. I got prayer a few times and the same thing happened every time. I started to believe that I wouldn't get healed from it. Then the pandemic hit and we were all to stay at home unless really needed to go out. After a while I noticed that my knee wasn't painful any longer. I paid attention to it, thinking it was going to come back but it didn't. I am healed. Not in my time but in God's time. When I let go and let God do the work that we had prayed for He was able to work and to heal me.

One Sunday morning in church Pastor Adam walked up to me while he was talking to the church and said, "Rita, the devil hates you." I could feel some of the people around me tense up. Being told something or someone hates you isn't nice but, in this case, it was a time for me to rejoice. He was and is right. I was glad that he recognized that the devil hated me because I hate him also. I am not to hate other people but it is OK to hate the devil. My spirit in me jumped for joy when I heard Pastor Adam saying it. It confirmed to me that I was doing something right. As far as I am concerned, it is my job to keep the devil hating me. If I do what God would have me do, which is follow what it says in His word (the Bible), then I will continue to achieve that feat. I know that when I follow what God wants me to do and am happy and joyful the devil doesn't like it and doesn't know what to do with me nor can he control me. This is a complete turnaround for me. You see, I no longer have control over anyone or anything, not that I really had it when I thought I did, except to follow Jesus and do what he wants. I do have the choice but I do choose to follow Jesus and have Him as my Lord and Saviour.

When Archie passed away, it was the worst thing in my life that has ever happened. I thought. But God, turned it into something good as He always does. I turned to Him for condolence and to face whatever came next in my life. When my brother-in-law died, my sister wanted to die and never did get on with her own life. I thought of that but somehow, I knew it wasn't what God had in store for me.

Looking back now, I decided to do the right thing and put my life in His hands the best I knew how. Because I turned to God my life is better today in ways I could never have imagined. "We get knocked down, but we are not destroyed," is the best way to describe what happened to me.

2 Corinthians 4:8-9 *8 We are pressed on every side by troubles, but we are not crushed. We are perplexed, but not driven to despair. 9 We are hunted down, but never abandoned by God. We get knocked down, but we are not destroyed.*

Step 6 says, "Were entirely ready to have God remove all these defects of character," and Step 7 says, "Humbly asked Him to remove our shortcomings." I got to these at different times since joining the Program depending on what I wanted to get rid of. I was very slow at one of my defects that I have been giving thought to for years and knew that what I was doing was very wrong and not only wrong but according to the Bible it is a sin. One night just before Holy Communion we were asked what we need to have cured or want to get rid of and I prayed to have it taken from me. That was only a few months ago as I write this. I thought I could handle it on my own after telling the church that I had something but wasn't really ready to talk about it yet. I said it again about couple of months ago and was told again to talk to one of the other women in the church about it. I did and it was very hard. I think it was the hardest of my secrets that I had to bring out in the light. I did talk about it to someone and found out that I wasn't alone. Thinking that I was alone doing it kept me in sin. I should have known better. If it is in the Bible not to do it then people have been doing it for centuries so why did I think I was alone in it? I really didn't want to quit doing it and wasn't ready to give it to God as the Step 7 says.

Secrets make us sick and I knew I had to talk about it to someone so I forced myself to. Knowing that God was grieved every time I did it. I was afraid to be judged but I wasn't. I believe now that God has healed and taken it all away as I have asked him. I had to be completely ready to change and let it go for good.

Doing the sin was the end result of what else I was doing beforehand and leading up to it. God made a way out for me many times but I ignored the way out and continued, knowing what I was about to do. The leading up wasn't the 'sin' but I knew that for me it was wrong because of the end result. Some people may say no it is not a sin nor is it wrong but at least for me it is very wrong.

As you can see, I am not where I need to be yet but I am not where I used to be. I still have a long way to go to be like God would have me be so I will continue to change for the better until I am ready to go Home.